DREAMS

a biblical model of interpretation

DREAMS

a biblical model of interpretation

Jim
Driscoll

Zach
Mapes

orbital
BOOK GROUP

This book is dedicated to Jesus Christ and His bride, the Church. This book was created to help all the dreamers in the world who hunger and long to know all of God's ways and won't stop until we are able, as a perfect and complete bride, to hear and understand all our Beloved longs to tell us.

—Jim Driscoll

This book is dedicated to Greg and Patty Mapes who have throughout my life shown me the faith and endurance in God that Job showed. It is as a direct result of their prayers, faith and example that I enjoy a living relationship with God and know for sure that He is real. Thank you.

—Zach Mapes

CONTENTS

DREAMS

a biblical model of interpretation

ACKNOWLEDGMENTS

JIM DRISCOLL —

Whenever you address a topic in a book that encapsulates a major section of your thoughts, there are so many people who have contributed to your thinking that it is hard to know where to begin acknowledging and where to end.

I won't begin with my kindergarten teacher, but I will begin with every teacher and adult who wanted to know what I was trying to communicate as a child, even if they couldn't fully grasp the abstract concepts I didn't quite have words for.

The wide group of patient and caring individuals who have provoked me to communicate better includes everybody, from Sunday school teachers to high school English teachers to my wife, Mims, and other friends I have had as an adult who wanted me to communicate my thoughts in clearer and more structured ways so what I desired to convey could be grasped.

The process in enabling clear, comprehendible language culminates with our editor, Lauren, who has again been able to transform my words into book form and yet still have them be my words.

In regard to the specific topic of dreams, there have been many provocateurs as well. I first think of all the dreamers whose great hunger and demand for understanding have helped pull this book out of me.

My introduction to dreams came at night in my sleep from God, as it did for all of you, even if you don't remember it. But my introduction to anointed, gifted, disciplined, and intentional dream interpretation came from people who had been redeveloping the language and concepts of biblical dream interpretation.

Of the men I know, Greg and John Paul have had a great impact on my development as an interpreter and teacher in the subject of dreams. Without men like these and others who came before them, I would probably be gifted in dream interpretation but unable to gain enough understanding to be of any significant use.

I would also like to acknowledge the great community of online dream interpreters it has been my privilege to interact with on a regular basis. They have been essential in provoking the questions that God has been faithful to respond to.

My co-author, Zach Mapes, has made tackling this huge topic much more feasible, comprehensive, and credible, not to mention a lot less lonely. I can think of no one else I would have written this book with, and without him, I wouldn't have even attempted to do so.

As for this book even existing at all, or being produced in a way that has made it happen in a year rather than a decade, I lay the chief blame and my great gratitude at the feet of our publisher, who has brought the elements of this book together like a composer with a great orchestra.

ZACH MAPES —

Firstly, to our publisher; thank you for the patience and long suffering you have shown us over the course of this book's development. Without your inspiration and sheer grit determination we certainly would not have been able to complete it.

A huge thank you to Lauren Stinton for the many hours of love and care you have put in with us to pull this book together. I hope you know we couldn't have done it without you. I would also like to thank those who read early drafts of the book, particularly Alice Goodwin Hudson for your valuable thoughts, contributions and encouragement.

A big thank you to all the churches and pastors I have worked with over the years; the experience and guidance I received from many of you has been invaluable. Thanks to my friends and colleagues who have encouraged and helped along the way Jonnie and Hannah Corrie, Alan and Diane McWilliams, Matt and Anita Fitzgerald, Steffen and Wendy Schulte, Kevin and Catherine Sforza.

To Doug and Larry White for all you have done to support my family.

To Steve, for integrity without measure; the church needs more friends like you.

To my wonderful mother-in-law Sylvia Lawson Johnston – thank you for giving us a home at a critical point in our journey, and to Andrew Lawson Johnston for having faith in a boy at a time when he had no hope

Most importantly of all to my wife, Tania, the love of my life and my best friend; I simply cannot imagine life without you – thank you.

I would also like to thank Jim for working with me on this book and helping make it such a worthwhile and memorable experience. It has been a highlight in a long friendship.

CHAPTER 1

WHY

DREAMS?

For God may speak in one way, or in another,
Yet man does not perceive it.
In a dream, in a vision of the night,
When deep sleep falls upon men,
While slumbering on their beds,
Then He opens the ears of men,
And seals their instruction.
— Job 33:14–16, NKJV

The mysteries of God are hidden in our dreams. The verse above tells us that as deep sleep falls God places instructions on our hearts. Do you want to know what your instructions are? Come with us, as we follow the examples of Joseph, Daniel, and others. This journey will release inspiration, understanding, and purpose that is locked away in your dreams just waiting for you to seek it out.

This is a book on dreams and their meanings written from a Christian, biblical prospective. Much of what we share in these pages is based on our experience and is substantiated directly and indirectly through Scripture. To grasp the basic precepts of this book, you need only be open to the possibility that a biblical God would speak to you and others through dreams.

Commonly defined, dreams are events seen in the mind while sleeping. That definition, though useful, does not capture the totality of what is going on when we are dreaming and later processing our dreams while awake. Dreams are not simply images and events that we experience during rest. They have the power to change our lives. They can reveal the answers that God has planted deep within each and every one of us, answers that are just waiting to be released, waiting to help us move closer to God and our destinies.

A few years ago, I (Zach) helped run a dream outreach at a large university student union. One of the people who approached us was a young guy just starting at the school. He, like many of the others present, had been drinking heavily. But as he began to tell us the recurring dream he had been having since starting school, we all felt a tangible peace that we knew to be the Spirit of God. The young man shared his dream with us:

I was walking down a long hallway away from bright lights toward a gray area, and beyond that was total darkness.

That was the entire dream, and our interpretation was just as simple. The dream was saying that his current direction in life was leading into total darkness, but it wasn't too late to turn his life around. Unprompted, and suddenly seeming sober, the young man got up from the table, left his drink behind, and said he felt it was time to go and pray.

That is the power of dreams. That is why we have written this book — to help you, and others, benefit from you dreams, in simple and yet profound ways.

When you start hearing about dreams, something triggers in your brain. We know many people who experienced a dramatic increase in their dream lives when they began to study how God communicates this way. Several of them said in the beginning that they didn't dream that often, or at all, but after being taught about dreams, or just being told that God can speak through dreams, they later contacted us to share how much their dream lives have changed. When presented with even a small understanding of how God speaks in dreams, it is as if the brain realizes, *Wait a minute. There's something here. Let me start paying attention to this.* When people have a revelation of the importance of dreams, they begin remembering their dreams or wanting to know what they mean. It is very possible — and probable — that as you read this book, the same will happen to you. You will likely see an incredible growth in your dream life simply because you are showing God that you have an interest in hearing from Him in your dreams.

For me (Zach), the importance of dreams is something that predates my memory. My parents are both very active dream interpreters, so for as long as I can recall, my family has been exploring the arena of dreams. They have always been something that is valued and given attention.

My parents came to faith at a large church in Rockwall,

Texas, where miraculous healings occurred very frequently and God was moving in other amazing ways. I have seen that level and intensity of power and visitation in only a couple of other places since then. In addition to the healings and other miracles that happened, there was something going on with dreams. It was accepted that dreams were important and you responded to them; they were valued. Since then, when living in more normalized environments where one doesn't typically see the power of God moving in the same outwardly dramatic manner, I have developed an even *greater* value for dreams, because I know God uses them to communicate with me during all seasons of life. Twenty-five years ago, dreams seemed to be only a small part of what He was doing. But now they are a large part of how I see Him moving, both in my life and the lives of the people around me. I think this is particularly true in the seasons of the still, small voice of God, when He can be hard to hear and seems difficult to find. Dreams often seem even more life changing in times like those.

The Bible talks about training children in the way they should go (Proverbs 22:6). I grew up with the understanding that dreams are a core form of divine communication. Because of that, I was able to circumvent a lot of the difficulty in learning to interpret them. In my experience researching and speaking about this subject, I look around at the adults who are just getting into dreams and sometimes struggling with the notion that God could be speaking to them in this way, and I am grateful for how many things seem natural to me simply because I grew up doing them. If you teach the concepts in this book to your children now, as they grow up, it will become second nature to them, rather than a potentially difficult task that requires rewiring of how they think. That rewiring can sometimes cause a literal, physical headache because in a sense, learning to think metaphorically is like bending your mind. But if you grow up with this understanding, some of these pathways will not need to be rewired; you will be able to interpret dreams and work through additional levels of metaphorical understanding in a way that seems more comfortable. Without my upbringing, I am sure I would have a totally different perspective on dreams.

Children have a natural affinity for dreams. Their interest will tend to come in phases; they might have dreams that seem irrelevant to them, or they might be really fascinated by them. But if they are introduced to the idea of dreams and dream interpretation at a young age, it definitely allows their natural mental and spiritual processes to grow and make room for God's interpretive process. They will have an easier time giving weight to dreams and learning to recognize the important messages from God that their dreams contain.

Though the approach is somewhat different, you can certainly learn to interpret dreams as an adult as well. Unlike Zach, I (Jim) didn't have much of a background or grid for dreams when I was growing up. I was raised in a mainline Protestant church, and I never gave much thought to them. In fact, it really wasn't until I was older and involved in prophetic ministry[1] that I realized I was ignoring almost all revelatory information that had any sort

---

1 Biblically based prophecy is the belief that God is still speaking to us today and the act of listening to what He is saying and potentially sharing this with others. This book addresses only the subset of prophecy that has to do with God speaking through dreams.

of metaphoric content to it. I was walking a tightrope of trying to hear prophetic words that were direct and perfectly clear: "This is what happened in your past. This is what will happen in your future. This is what God is saying." Anything that needed any kind of interpretation — pictures I was seeing, words that weren't literal or needed me to spend time with God in order to understand — I was ignoring in order to have clean, straightforward messages from Him. If I woke up from a metaphorical dream, such as walking through a field of flowers, I would think, *There is no clear message from God here, so it must not be important.* I believed that dreams could be from God, but I didn't understand that dreams, even the "weird" ones, could be interpreted, and God would give me understanding about them.

Then came a sudden realization: *This could be telling me something that's from God, and when I interpret it, it could be more relevant and powerful than the revelation I was receiving that didn't need an interpretation.* That woke me up, if you pardon the pun. It opened the floodgates to many things. I realized there were all these revelatory elements that I had been ignoring.

For me, discovering dreams was like jumping into cold water. It was an intense immersion, not a gradual growing up in them as it was with Zach. I went from completely ignoring them to being completely engrossed in them, and in some ways, it was a shock to my system. I can remember times when I was interpreting a dream, and it felt like the inside of my brain was melting. I would literally feel heat coming off my head, and it seemed to me that I couldn't interpret this dream because I didn't think the right way. So as I did interpret it, my brain changed. It adjusted for the revelation. Afterward, I would feel exhausted and I would need to recover physically and mentally. Over time, this process happens less frequently and I recover more quickly, because it seems that I no longer need to have my thought process drastically altered with every new dream I encounter.

I now recognize the dazed look on people's faces when they are just discovering dreams. God spoke to them; they received revelation from Him, and it altered the way their brain handles information. Their minds feel different because they *are* different. People will sit there in a fog as I explain, "No, you'll be okay. Your brain is just working. It is being transformed by the Spirit. You're training the mind to think in ways it isn't used to."

WHY DREAMS?

We have told you how we became interested in dreams. The reason we *stay* interested is that we see an incredible value in them. We consistently see dreams impacting people in a way that is positive and life changing.

How will dreams impact you? They are important and constructive on a few different levels. For one, they affect how we deal with strongholds and opinions that we are not prepared to resolve. I (Zach) used to work in the restaurant industry, and I thought I was going to do that until I retired. But then I had a series of dreams that began to tell me that my time in the restaurant business conflicted with the kind of spiritual relationships I desired. Had I received that same revelation during a time of ministry or while praying or going about my daily life, I may not have heard it at all simply because I wasn't open to that specific revelation. I needed a dream to push through my preconceived ideas and plans.

When information, correction, or direction comes through a dream, it can slip through the natural opinions, defenses, and strongholds we have and speak truth to our hearts. God will often use dreams to bring change to our points of view, beliefs, and intentions. It might be that He will reveal times ahead so that we will rethink our plans and goals. When we are awake, there are some ideas that are almost too radical for us to have. They could be too offensive to our notions or ideas of the world, and our personal opinions prevent them from settling within us and becoming "tangible" in our minds. So dreams can sidestep our own understanding and reveal the understanding of God. They are one of the ways that God uses to keep us on track.

I (Jim) have had several dreams in which God clearly rebuked me. I've also had dreams that God has "interrupted" to tell me that what I'm doing in the dream is wrong. For instance, I once had a dream in which I was playing American football with some of my coworkers. Every time I got the ball, I didn't even have to run; I would simply walk toward the end zone and get a touchdown. Later as we were sitting on the bleachers, the coaches started talking about how they were going to organize the league and change some of the rules. I became upset.

"You're not playing," I said. "You're coaching. How come you get to change the rules? How come we, the ones who are playing, don't get to decide on the rules?" I meant myself — I was the one scoring.

The moment I said that in the dream, I heard loudly in my head, "Sedition." I realized the thoughts I was having were rebellious, and I woke up and started repenting. I immediately knew what the dream was about. I had been speaking against a decision made at work and was wondering why my bosses hadn't spoken to the staff about it first.

So dreams can cut through the barriers that keep us from being able to see our actions the way God sees them. This means they can address subtle issues that may be culturally acceptable but are actually offensive in God's eyes.

Second, dreams are infinitely valuable because they deepen the mystery of who God is. God is infinite. It will take all of eternity to know Him, as Scripture says:

> For we know in part and we prophesy in part;
> but when the perfect comes, the partial will be
> done away.
> When I was a child, I used to speak like a child,
> think like a child, reason like a child; when I be-
> came a man, I did away with childish things.
> For now we see in a mirror dimly, but then face to
> face; now I know in part, but then I will know fully
> just as I also have been fully known.
> — 1 Corinthians 13:9–12

Dreams perpetually show us that there is more to God than we currently comprehend. We can read His Word and feel that we have a good grasp on it; we can have a set theology in our minds and think we really understand the ways of Heaven and God's nature. But then we have a dream, and we realize there are *plenty* of things we don't understand yet.

Take, for example, the trance Peter had in Acts 10, where he saw a number of animals, reptiles, and birds being let down to the Earth on a large sheet. This spiritual experience changed his whole theology, and he realized Jesus' message was for the Gentiles as well as the Jews. God will use circumstances in our lives to unsettle our assumptions about Him, but the process can be faster and much easier for us if He also uses dreams.

Dreams can reveal that He is so much more amazing than we realized; underneath the water, the iceberg goes far deeper and wider than what we perceived on the surface. In the same way, dreams from God can be *mysterious*, because He is so profound. There may be times when we realize we don't yet know enough about Him to interpret a certain dream. Understanding a dream can sometimes mean that we need to understand God in ways that we currently cannot comprehend.

Along with that, you will find that some dreams and some interpretations are more of an investment of time and energy than others. Some dreams we will be able to understand fairly quickly or even interpret them while we're having them, but other dreams require continued discipline and a good deal of revelation. And as we mature in our interpretive gifts, we will be invited deeper into the mysteries of God hidden in dreams. Why? Because it is "the glory of God to conceal a matter, but the glory of kings is to search out a matter" (Proverbs 25:2). This applies to dreams in an extraordinary way. As we get better at metaphorical understanding and interpretation, God tends to hide more and more of Himself in our dreams. He includes elements[2] and symbols[3] that are harder to interpret because He's inviting us deeper into the mystery of who He is.

In our experience, you never master having dreams, interpreting dreams, hearing God, or sharing prophetically. God perpetually invites His children to grow.

DREAMS PRODUCE HUNGER FOR GOD

Dreams initiate a hunger for God within us. They show us the light behind the curtain, and they put a longing within us to draw the curtain back and see what has been hidden on the other side.

This hunger is the best and healthiest way for people to become interested in dreams. They are pricked with a desire to know more of God and how He speaks. Perhaps they had dreams from Him and they sense they mean something they don't yet understand, or perhaps the *idea* of dreams draws them in, and they want to know how they can get better at remembering and interpreting them. This can start to happen before they know who God is or have a developed belief in Him. People can become interested in dreams for a variety of reasons, but if their motivation

---

2 *Each individual object in a dream*

3 Something that represents or stands for something else (a material object representing something abstract)

is healthy, there is hunger for God in it. This is true with any activity or practice in life; if it is healthy, it will draw us closer to God.

At times, this hunger seems to hit people especially hard when their dreams are interpreted using methods that don't take into account the heart of God that the dreamer's spirit senses was in the dream. The main difference between those methods and what we are presenting in this book is that they do not account for an external source, namely God. They are focused on revealing internal issues. These methodologies may lead to the understanding of certain *pieces* of dreams but do not address the core concern of God's heart for the dreamer. The premise of these methodologies is simply that we are essentially the source of our dreams, whether they are internal or external. This is all part of what can broadly be defined as a humanist approach to dreams — an approach that, if adhered to, leaves no room for God. However, when God's heart starts to be revealed to dreamers, the hunger to know more sets in.

We know dozens of stories of people who caught a glimpse of His heart and just couldn't stay away from it. I (Zach) remember teaching a dream course at a church with my dad, and a woman attended who was not a Christian. She was a member of a New Age community,[4] but she had come across some of the dream outreaches I'd been running, and she attended the course because her dream's interpretation had profoundly affected her. She didn't care that the event was a Christian event; she just wanted to get closer to what was going on, and she ended up coming

---

4 A community of people who engage in various spiritual practices but do not adhere to Christian doctrine

to faith in Christ.

Dreams that have not been correctly interpreted will often stay with the dreamer. They are like the key on your key chain that you don't recognize; you have no idea what lock it goes to, but you know you don't want to throw it away, just in case.

A few years ago, I (Jim) was part of a team doing dream interpretations at a bookstore. A man came up to us and said, "I don't need a dream interpretation. I already know what this dream means, but I'll share it with you because I don't have anything better to do." He then shared a dream he'd had when he was about seven years old. The essence of the dream was that he was a crystalline statue that had been smashed with a hammer.

The situation was somewhat humorous because on the one hand, he was saying, "This is no big deal. I've taken psychology classes, and I already know what this means. I just want to share it." But on the other hand, he was sharing a dream that was twenty to thirty years old, and it was clear that it carried some unresolved emotional content for him. God gave me the interpretation so clearly, and I was able to tell him that the dream was about the emotional impact his father's words were having on him when he was just a boy. He almost broke down in tears.

Dreams pierce you. They help you realize that despite all your preconceptions, there is more to God than what you were expecting. In some ways, it seems that many people who are "hooked" by God-led dream interpretation can start out with all the false beliefs or notions they want, because once they've had a taste of the true impact of God, they can't settle for anything other than Him. All their false assumptions eventually fade away in His light.

Dreams can start people on a lifelong journey to find God and discover how He speaks, and this journey can be hard to derail because they have had a taste of it. They've had just enough to realize, *This is real. There is something here. Let me find out if God really gave me that dream because I cannot account for the way the interpretation has impacted me.*

OUR HEART WITH THIS BOOK

Our main goal in writing this book is to help people who are interested in dreams continue down that path in a way that will help them grow, avoid dead ends, and stay away from the subjective, make-up-whatever-you-want attitudes that exist in many religious arenas. It is our heart to see dream interpreters grow in their skills and learn the language of God, of which dreams are a part.

Both of us have been teaching and speaking on biblical dream interpretation for many years, and we have seen a great impact on the people we have worked with. Through working together, we have defined a comprehensive interpretive process. Because we must call it something, internally we call our process the Mapes/Driscoll interpretive framework. It is meant to be an open framework that allows, through consistency and discipline, the correct interpretation to be uncovered with revelation and discernment. By doing this, we do not mean to claim that our way is the only way to interpret dreams, or that all ideas and concepts were ours originally, but we can say that we have not seen all of these ideas and concepts presented together in this way.

We want to give the Church a reference point. We want you to be able to read this book and know you are reading an *introduction* to the theory of dream interpretation that is based on what we've learned from biblical study, practice, observation, and various mentors. It is a refined culmination of different models. This book is not meant to be a complete answer; it is meant to be a building block — something that can serve as a foundation as you grow in your own process and discover what works best for you.

By creating a model that is easy to reference, we hope to give pastors, elders, and other leaders within churches and communities common ground with dreamers and interpreters. This book offers a uniform vocabulary and a common reference point so that the Church can have support and encouragement and a better idea of how to approach the subject of dreams.

The necessity for clarity on vocabulary relating to dreams is similar to the need for that same uniformity in other fields of study. If two people are talking about the same thing, but using different words to describe that concept, it can cause quite a bit of confusion. I (Zach) was recently with some friends in Scotland. While we were getting ready to head off, one of the guys said we needed to grab the "cart." A few minutes later, our truck stopped and picked up a trailer. That is not what a "cart" means in my vocabulary. Had I been sent off to accomplish this task on my own, something else would have happened. A common vocabulary is very important and can help alleviate confusion.

As you go through this book, be prepared. You are opening a door to the spiritual realm, and what is on the other side will amaze you and have great impact on your life and relationship with God.

CHAPTER 2

THE BIBLICAL BASIS
FOR DREAM INTERPRETATION

In Genesis 20, a pagan king named Abimelech had a dream. In the dream, God appeared to him, and Abimelech very quickly and without protest made some decisions based on what God told him in his dream.

This is the first reference to dreams in Scripture. In all, the Bible contains about two hundred stories of or references to dreams. People had dreams, interpreted these dreams, and made life decisions based on their dreams.

One detail stands out in each of these biblical dream stories: None of the dreamers seemed surprised that God would speak to them this way, or that they would make decisions centered around what they had dreamt. Based on the prevalence of dreams and the responses biblical characters had to them, it would appear that hearing from God in this way was not something new or out of the ordinary. It was a frequent occurrence in their lives, or it had happened enough in the cultures mentioned in Scripture as a whole that it didn't surprise them.

Throughout the Bible, it is clear that dreams were one of the most common ways in which God communicated to His people. In particular, dreams are distinctly central to Jesus' parents and others in and around His life. In Matthew 1:20, Joseph was told in a dream that he should continue in his plan to wed Mary, his betrothed, even though she was unexpectedly pregnant and he was not the father. This, clearly, was a new idea for him, but the fact that he made a life-changing decision based on a dream was not the point that he struggled with. This shows a value of dreams that countless people would have a hard time accepting and carrying out in many present-day cultures. We can see the influence dreams had in Joseph's world as he was obedient in a very difficult and embarrassing situation. Later on, it was again through a dream that Joseph took his family to safety in Egypt, and through another dream, he was told when it was safe to return to Israel. When Jesus' young life was on the line, God chose to convey His direction through dreams.

We again see the influence of dreams in the story of the Wise Men (Matthew 2:12) and later with Pilate's wife (Matthew 27:19), who was not a follower of Jesus as far as we know. It seems to be almost taken for granted in Scripture that if someone had a dream, he or she was going to listen to it.

From Genesis to Revelation, there was a cultural understanding that people would have dreams and they should pay serious attention to those dreams. We see this not just among the biblical scholars of the time such as Daniel, but also among non-Jewish people (Abimelech, Pharaoh, etc.). This is important to understand because in many modern cultures, the opposite seems to be true. If someone were to consider making a decision based on a dream in modern western society, it generally would be seen as a novel if not ridiculous notion. However, for the characters in Scripture, the men and women we attempt to emulate, this was not the case. On the contrary, heeding dreams seemed to be quite natural and common.

As we lay a foundation for our understanding of dream interpretation, we first want to look at the basis for it in Scripture. We have tried to ensure that the precedents found in this book are sufficiently based on biblical accounts and a theological understanding of specific verses.

We will also be looking at the Hebrew language itself as a basis for dream interpretation. In its ancient form, Hebrew is pictographic, similar to Chinese characters and Egyptian hieroglyphics. Each root word is composed of at least two pictures, and each of those pictures represents something tangible that has symbolic meaning. When viewed as a whole, therefore, the word brings a deep and intricate understanding to the idea it represents, and each word can have several meanings based on the context in which it is found.

The meanings of these ancient words remain fairly consistent throughout the evolution of the Hebrew language. In effect, what we can see metaphorically in the ancient Hebrew characters supports what we can read in modern translations of Hebrew.[1]

For instance, *Ab*[2] is translated as "father." It is comprised of the Hebrew character *Alef*, which is an ox head, and the Hebrew character *Bet*, which is a tent. The ox is understood to represent strength, and the tent is understood to symbolize the family, so a father is the strong one of the tent or family. These two characters also refer to the strong center pole that holds up the tent, showing the metaphoric role of the father in the Hebraic culture. Similarly, the word for *mother* is comprised of the characters for water (*Mem*) and the ox head, which together mean "strong water." The same word is used for *glue* and shows the mother's metaphoric role of holding the family together.

How do we know we can use Scripture as the basis for dream interpretation? Paul wrote in 2 Timothy 3:16–17 that all Scripture is "inspired by God and profitable for teaching, for reproof, for correction, for training in righteousness," so that the people of God may be complete and equipped for every good work. Godly dream interpretation can certainly be considered a good work as it *requires* biblical understanding, knowledge of the ways and nature of God, and a deepening relationship with Him.

Biblical dream interpretation differs from secular models of dream interpretation by accepting the fact that dreams can come from a source beyond ourselves. More often than not, other models work on the assumption that our dreams are our subconscious speaking to us *about* ourselves. Yes, dreams are a natu-

---

1 Benner, *The Ancient Hebrew Language and Alphabet: Understanding the Ancient Hebrew Language of the Bible Based on Ancient Hebrew Culture and Thought*. Please refer to the bibliography at the end of this book for more information.
2 *Strong's H1*

ral, God-created method of processing information, but based on Scripture, we can see that not all dreams are from our subconscious alone.

Much of this book's foundation will be pulled from those two precedents: Scripture itself and the ancient Hebrew language, in which the Old Testament was primarily written. Theologically speaking, everything we will be discussing in this book is based on what the Bible says and the literal and metaphoric translation of the words it uses. We will also include examples based on history, current studies, and personal experience.

We related some of our history in dreams and dream interpretation in the first chapter. Our experience has been that when correctly understood, dreams are a crucial key to following God. The best part is that we are daily learning and growing in our own understanding of dreams and who God made us to be. All of this is a process that doesn't end.

SCRIPTURAL PRECEDENTS FOR DREAM INTERPRETATION

Scripture is filled with precedents that serve as our basis for dream interpretation. First, with Abimelech we can see that even people who are not known as followers of God can have dreams, ones that they know they need to respond to (Genesis 20).

Abimelech took Sarah, Abraham's wife, and after he had done so, God told him in a dream he was going to die because of his actions. When Abimelech woke up, he gave Sarah back to

Abraham and made absolutely certain he did everything he could to ensure that he and Abraham were on good terms. This is a clear example of someone responding to a dream by making changes in his or her waking life. And it is also an example of God's grace!

Later in Genesis 37, we find another precedent. This is the first time that we see a response to a metaphoric dream. When Joseph was a boy, he had dreams that were metaphoric in nature and required interpretation in order to understand. He shared those dreams with his brothers. That, however, didn't work out well for him, and he ended up in slavery due to his brothers' jealously. So we also see from this story the importance of being wise when we share our dreams with those around us, even if they are close friends or family. It is interesting to note that though Joseph's brothers were not enthused about his dreams, they seemed to agree with the implied interpretation of them (that Joseph would be a leader and they would bow down to him).

Joseph sets another precedent a few chapters later when he interpreted the dreams of the butler and baker in prison (Genesis 40). He is the first person we see who interpreted someone else's dream in a way that enabled the dreamer to understand what God was saying. The butler and baker had dreams, and in the process of interpreting them, Joseph told them that dreams and interpretations are from God — i.e, he told them that this was what God was saying to them. Then, not only were his interpretations accurate, but we can see that it was right for him to interpret their dreams in the first place; it was good for the dreamers to know what God was saying. By implication, God *wanted* them to know the meaning of what they were dreaming.

That story is the first scriptural example in which we see people relying on someone else's interpretation in order to understand their dreams. Joseph had a relationship with God and a refined gift in this area, and through his interpretations, the dreamers were informed of God's plan.

Joseph's ability to interpret dreams and the dreamer's desire to hear and believe his interpretations are illustrated again when Joseph is brought to interpret Pharaoh's dreams (Genesis 41). In that instance, we see a person interpreting dreams for someone in power and authority simply because that person is in power and authority. The precedent suggests that there will be times when the dreams of leaders need to be interpreted so that they can make good decisions. Joseph interpreted Pharaoh's dreams, and Pharaoh made good decisions for a large number of people based on what Joseph told him.

Several centuries later as Daniel interpreted Nebuchadnezzar's dream of the tree (Daniel 4), he exemplified many of these same elements. In that example, Nebuchadnezzar, a non-Jew and the leader of his people, had a dream. He shared that dream with someone who had a close relationship with God and knew how to interpret dreams, and the leader learned what God was saying and then responded.

As we can see, the lives of Joseph and Daniel establish several precedents for people who have a relationship with God and are gifted, trained, called, competent, and credible to help other people understand their dreams. In fact, we can see quite clearly in Joseph's story that, where it is helpful, we can and *should* interpret dreams for others and that the dreamers can and should make decisions influenced by those interpretations. Just as important is the fact that when properly equipped, we can understand our own dreams as well.

Again, it is evident that interpreting dreams is not a new concept. It is a biblically established occurrence. If someone in the Bible had a dream from God, he or she made changes or took actions based on the meaning of that dream.

These stories are our prototypes not only for receiving dreams from God but for interpreting them and then potentially, if we are capable and trained, helping others with their dreams so they can know what God is saying to them as well. In our experience, God will often create circumstances to prompt you to interpret other people's dreams.

DREAMS THROUGHOUT HISTORY

Having built a clear foundation from Scripture for dream interpretation, we can see how dreams have continued to influence relationship with God, the Church, and the world throughout the rest of history. For example, many important characters in the early Church had dreams that impacted their lives, from warning them of the future to helping them reach their destinies:

- Polycarp (69–155) dreamt he would be martyred in Rome.[3]
- Josephus (in 66) was inspired to lead the Jew-

---

3 Cave, A Complete History of the Lives, Acts, and Martyrdoms of Those Who Were Contemporary with, or Immediately succeeded, the Apostles: Volume 2.

ish army against the Romans due to a dream.[4]

- Justin Martyr (100–165) was guided by dreams.[56]

- Tertullian (160–220) said, "It is to dreams that the greater part of the human race owe their knowledge of God."[7]

- Irenaeus (125–200) considered dreams to be his contact with God.[8]

- Origen (185–254) used dreams to understand his faith.[9]

- Dionysius of Alexandria (pope of Alexandria from 248–265) walked in his destiny because of a dream.[10]

- St. Augustine (354–430) referenced dreams as an important way God communicated with humanity.[11]

- St. Jerome (340–420), who translated the Bible into the Latin vulgate, was converted through a dream.[12]

- St. Thomas of Aquinas (1225–1274) depended

---

4 Gnuse, *Dreams and Dream Reports in the Writings of Josephus: A Traditio-Historical Analysis*

5 Kelsey, *God, Dreams, and Revelation: A Christian Interpretation of Dreams*

6 Osborn, *Justin Martyr*

7 Savary, Berne, and Williams; *Dreams and Spiritual Growth: A Judeo-Christian Way of Dreamwork*

8 Irenaeus, *The Treatise of Irenæus of Lugdunum Against the Heresies (v.2): A Translation of the Principal Passages, With Notes and Arguments.*

9 Miller, *Dreams in Late Antiquity: Studies in the Imagination of a Culture*

10 Robertson, *History of the Christian Church to the Pontificate of Gregory the Great, A.D. 590*

11 Kelsey, *God, Dreams, and Revelation: A Christian Interpretation of Dreams*

12 Bulkeley, *Visions of the Night: Dreams, Religion, and Psychology*

on dreams and visions to write his works.[13]

That is just a glimpse of the great importance the early Christian fathers gave to dreams — an importance that many Christians today do not think to give them. From modern history until now, dreams have continued to play a significant role in the lives of people who are influencing the world in secular, political, and scientific arenas:

- Elias Howe dreamt he was being attacked by people with spears. The nature of the spears resolved an issue he'd had with the design of his sewing machine.[14]

- Abraham Lincoln had a dream during his first term that said he would be killed near the end of his second. He also had a recurring dream that would come to him before important historical events took place.[15]

- Otto Loewi (1873–1961), a German-born physiologist, won the Nobel Prize for medicine in 1936 for his work on chemical transmission, of which he came to a deeper understanding in a dream.[16]

- Jack Nicklaus, a famous golfer, discovered his swing in a dream in 1964. He was trying to im-

---

13 Savary, Berne, and Williams; Dreams and Spiritual Growth: A Judeo-Christian Way of Dreamwork

14 Krippner, Extraordinary Dreams and How to Work with Them

15 Lamon, Recollections of Abraham Lincoln

16 Bear, Neuroscience: Exploring the Brain

prove his game, and his dream eventually led to
what became the modernization of golf. [17]

- The song *Yesterday* came to Paul McCartney in
  a dream in 1965. [18] [19]

Clearly, dreams have had a significant influence in the lives
and stories of history. But what has caused the Western World to
lose much of its appreciation of dreams?

During the Reformation, the emerging Protestant Church
attempted to counter the legacy of the Roman Catholic Church
by constraining its theological doctrine to biblical precedent and
ignoring mystical experiences. Intended or not, a result of this was
a Protestant society that had lost its mystical heritage, including
that of accepting the possibility of God-inspired dreams and their
interpretations. The Enlightenment continued the questioning of
de facto beliefs by putting everything that was believed into question, not just the mystical heritage of the Catholic Church but every part of European society.

The Western World has never fully recovered from this.
Today, many people hold to the work of Carl Jung, Fritz Perls, Sig-
mund Freud, and other humanistic models that attribute dreaming solely to the psychological arena. These models internalize
dreams and don't leave room for the possibility that they could be
influenced and even produced by outside sources, and so for several generations, what is perceived as reliable or scientific dream

---

17 *Jack Nicklaus, as told to a San Francisco Chronicle reporter; June 27, 1964*
18 *Spignesi and Lewis, Here, There, and Everywhere: The 100 Best Beatles Songs*
19 *Cryer, Love Me Tender: The Stories Behind the World's Best-loved Songs*

interpretation has rested primarily in the hands of individuals who are not looking to God for insight. These models produce interpretations that often do not resonate with the dreamer; rather, they reinforce issues that were uncovered in therapy sessions. These humanistic models place humanity at the head rather than God, and thus are bound to fall short.

It is important to note, however, that not every aspect of this psychological rationalization has been negative. It has actually helped to provide some trails for those who pay attention to their dreams but are unaware that it is God who is speaking to them. Dreams can penetrate secular circles and influence people who would oppose them if they realized they were hearing from or about God. As they don't feel the need to attribute dreams to Him, they are more open to hearing from Him in this way.

We understand that several modern models of interpretation, specifically those of psychological and New Age origins (such as Freudian, Gestalt, and Jungian), may have some value in them and in certain areas may even partially agree with biblical models of interpretation. However, we do not believe these models are good or beneficial as the basis for godly dream interpretation. We reference some of them for terminology and historical information but are not necessarily suggesting them for further reading. It can be confusing to spend much time looking at emotional and soul-based models while trying to interpret dreams from a biblical standpoint. Instead, God has laid out clear examples of how we can interpret dreams in His Word.

CHAPTER 3

DREAMS AND
UNDERSTANDING METAPHORS

Why are dreams important? For those who are seeking after God, the primary reason is that we want more of Him in our lives. We want to know the way He speaks. We want to know what He says, *how* He says it, and *why*. Hopefully, as you go through this book and spend time with your dreams, you will see not only an increase in your dream life, but an increase in the most important thing any of us could have: relationship with God.

The Bible makes it clear that God is more than we could ever think of or imagine. His thoughts are not our thoughts, His ways not our ways (Isaiah 55:8–9). What does this mean for dreams? Dreams from God make us ask questions and help us to see ourselves in new and different ways. They help us see facets of who we are now and who we are meant to be. Dreams also show us the ways, nature, and various aspects of God that we may have never understood before.

How do they do this? God often helps us understand Him by communicating to us through things that we do not initially comprehend. In many cases, He uses metaphors. A metaphor is defined as a figure of speech in which a word or description is applied to an object to which it is not literally related. For example, when God refers to Himself in Scripture as a lion or a lamb, He is revealing that there are similarities between His nature and the natures of those animals. When He speaks about Himself through metaphors, He is essentially saying, *This object or action is like Me. When you understand the similarities, you will understand Me at a greater level.* By using metaphors that can be correctly understood only through revelation and relationship with Him, He is inviting us to come in and know Him better.

A few years ago, I (Jim) was practicing communicating with God, and I asked Him, "What is going to happen today?"

I sensed Him reply, "Things are going to start making lots and lots of sense. Lots of change is coming."

All that day, I looked to see change in my life, but nothing happened. I didn't see any change at all. In the evening, I went back to Him and said, "You said lots of change was coming, but nothing changed today."

"Reach into your left-hand pocket," He replied.

I did — and suddenly realized how full of change it was. In each store I had visited that day, I had received several coins back from the cashier. My purchases had consistently totaled to $2.02 or $5.17 or similar amounts that had returned lots of quarters, dimes, nickels, and pennies. I now had a pocketful of change that added up to a lot of cents.

I had been looking to see "change" (some sort of modification in my circumstances) and for things to make sense (a clear understanding of things going on), and when nothing happened, I questioned whether or not I had heard Him correctly. But I had heard Him correctly; He had been using a pun, a play on words, and through it, He was training me to understand the way He speaks through metaphors.

In this chapter, we will be discussing the nature of metaphors: what they are, how we should interpret them, and what they have to do with dreams. We will begin by looking at the metaphorical nature of Scripture.

METAPHORS IN SCRIPTURE

The Bible, as the Word of God, is full of metaphors, and those metaphors need to be interpreted in order for us to understand what God is saying. If we don't do this, we end up facing enigmas we won't be able to easily understand, which happened to Nicodemus in John 3. He was responsible for teaching all of Israel about God, but there were certain aspects that he himself didn't grasp.

When Jesus told him, "You have to be born again," Nicodemus tried to interpret that literally.

"How can any man go back to his mother's womb?" he asked.

But Jesus was using a metaphor. *Birth* can be a metaphorical representation of the spiritual process of coming to salvation — of being born again.

As we just mentioned, in John 1:36, Jesus is portrayed as a lamb. In **Revelation 5:5**, He is portrayed as a lion. These metaphors display His attributes in a way that helps us see Him as He is. If we didn't know to interpret them, we would not have as complete a picture of God.

These are just a few examples of how we cannot understand much of Scripture without understanding metaphors, puns, and other forms of poetic language. In the same way, we cannot understand the dreams God gives us if they stay encrypted. Some dreams are literal, but most contain metaphorical content, so in order to know what God is communicating to us, we need to grow in this area.

METAPHORS IN ANCIENT HEBREW

Hebrew-based languages are the only languages we see God writing with His own hand in Scripture. With Moses on Mount Sinai, He wrote the Ten Commandments twice. He wrote *Mene, Mene, Tekel, Parsin* on the wall in Babylon; these were Aramaic (closely related to Hebrew) words that Daniel translated in Daniel 5:25–28. Aramaic or Hebrew is presumably the language Jesus used when He wrote in the sand in John 8:6.

God used ancient Hebrew as the language of the Pentateuch and as a foundation for the rest of the Old Testament. In other words, He chose it to serve as the basis for the coming of His Son and the salvation of all people.

When I (Jim) first began to discover for myself the metaphorical richness of ancient Hebrew, I was studying the Hebrew word *Shem*, which means "name". In the ancient Hebrew characters, it is composed of a picture of teeth and a picture of water.

How can teeth and water represent a person's name? I wondered.

As a metaphor, teeth typically represent understanding because we "chew" on something in order to process it. Water can represent the Spirit (John 4:13–14) or a mystery (it covers and hides things of depth; we can see the surface of the ocean much more easily than we can see all it contains).

As I thought about these two metaphors together, I began to realize what God was actually saying with this word. A name represents a person's essence, the understanding of the mystery of who he or she is. Each of the words I have studied in ancient Hebrew is like this. Some have very practical meanings, and some have very profound meanings.

HEBRAIC UNDERSTANDING OF "DREAM" AND "INTERPRET"

When we look at the pictographs used in *dream* and *interpret* in the ancient Hebrew language, we will have a better understanding of what is actually happening as we dream and what we are doing as we interpret those dreams.

"DREAM" IN *ANCIENT HEBREW*

The Hebrew word for "dream" is *chalowm*, which is composed of four different pictures: a wall, a staff, a tent peg, and water.

The picture of a wall represents a division or separation: something beyond the divider. Scripture uses this picture of the tent wall in Genesis 1 when God is putting the firmament in place to separate the seas below and the seas above.

The staff can represent authority, but more specifically, it could mean something that is being brought to you. The symbol for water represents mystery or the Spirit, and the tent peg means "joined together," or something that holds things together.

When we consider these symbols collectively, we see that the word *dream* in ancient Hebrew can mean that the mystery on the other side of the wall is being brought to you. It is passing before you, and as that happens, you perceive a mystery — that is, you catch a glimpse of what is transpiring in the spiritual realm. Whatever happens on the other side of that divider could be what you are seeing in your dream: the decrees of God, the mind of God, the future, the past, hidden knowledge, wisdom, healing, and much more.

This is important to understand because the Hebrew word for "dream" does not say that while we sleep, we have thoughts, memories, or experience simply a psychological process. Instead, it says that while we sleep, we draw close to the mysteries of the Spirit, and we perceive some of them. Every time we say, "I had a dream last night," we are actually saying, "I came close to a spiritual mystery." We are not merely sharing the pictures we saw while asleep.

"INTERPRET" IN ANCIENT HEBREW

Sometimes dreams will be clear, or literal. For instance, when God told Abimelech that he was about to die in Genesis 20:3, the meaning of the dream was unmistakable. When God told Joseph to take Mary and Jesus into Egypt (Matthew 2:13), that dream was also clear. But in our experience, most often "what passes before us" is not immediately understandable, such as the Midianite dream about the barley loaf that Gideon heard in Judges 7:13–14. It contains mysteries that need to be interpreted.

There are two Hebrew words used in the Bible for "interpret." One is *pathar*, which is used when Joseph interpreted a dream, for example. It is comprised of pictures of a mouth (the opening of something), a cross (a symbolic marker), and a head (the beginning or the "head" of something, as in leadership).

The other variation for *interpret* is *pashar*, which is used when Nebuchadnezzar was searching for an interpretation to his dream. It is also formed with a mouth and a head, but instead of a cross, it has a picture of teeth (which can signify understanding or processing something).

So when we *pathar* a dream, we're opening up the symbols of the dream, and when we *pashar* a dream, we're opening up the understanding inside the dream. They are parallel meanings in the sense that they are opening up hidden meanings of a dream's symbols. The mysteries of the Spirit are being brought into our influence, and when they are interpreted, we are opening up the veil or mystery; we are seeing what the symbols in the dream mean.

After you have been interpreting for a while, you recognize that you often are interpreting a dream by explaining the meaning of the metaphors it contains. That is what the actual Hebrew words say you are doing. You are "making open" the symbols of a dream. This needs to be done in context with the dream as a whole, as we will discuss in the following section.

METAPHORS AND CONTEXT

Again, true metaphorical understanding requires a real relationship with God. It is important to rely on the Holy Spirit during the interpretive process because discerning context plays a huge role in what a metaphor may mean in a dream. A certain symbol may have a certain meaning in one dream and have a very different meaning in another dream.

The word *kindness* is a good example of multiplicity in meaning. Depending on the context, the pictographs symbolizing "kindness" can also mean "rejection"! Context plays a huge role in the interpretation. The Hebrew word for "kindness" is *chasad* and is comprised of the following characters: ‏חסד. The first character is a tent wall and signifies a barrier. The second character is a bunch of thorns, which would indicate that the barrier is guarded. The third character is a tent doorway, meaning an entrance. It is kindness to open a door in a protected barrier and let someone in, and it is rejection to close the door. This is an example of multiplicity of metaphors in context. All metaphors can have positive, neutral, and negative connotations based on the context of the given dream.

It is also important to remember that how you interpret

the connotations of a metaphor may depend greatly on your own perspective. An example of this is the President of the United States or the Prime Minister of Britain. If the person you voted for is not in power, it is very possible that you have negative feelings about the current leader. I remember talking with some friends back when Tony Blair was the Prime Minister of the United Kingdom and being totally shocked at how negative they were. As an American, I don't have a strong pull toward either political party, so my position was very neutral. If you were to dream about a political leader, the person could represent several different things that may or may not align with your political leanings. And if you were to interpret a similar dream for someone else, it could have a very different meaning entirely.

One of the simplest examples I can recall of a metaphor meaning different things to different people happened when I was teaching a dream workshop. A woman had had a dream about being out at night and having a large black dog walking beside her. It is easy to assume that this would be a negative symbol. Before the woman continued to share her dream, many in the class had already made up their minds that this was a dark and scary dream, and the dog represented something bad. For some people, dogs are not friendly symbols. This may be because they were attacked by a dog at a young age or any number of reasons. But on the other hand, a dog is known as "man's best friend," and that is how many people feel about them.

God knows us. He knows our fears and our history. He may use dream symbols in a personal way. This is what we call a *personal dream vocabulary*. It is composed of symbols that have special meaning to us, or symbols that we repeatedly see in our own dreams that have had consistent or established meaning.

Not long ago, my wife and I (Zach) experienced a massive snowstorm in the Highlands of Scotland. Surveying the pristine white landscape brought some different metaphors to mind: beauty, a complete covering, the purity of the landscape, and — most notably in my context — not being able to get up the driveway without a 4x4. If I had this scene in a dream, the snow could potentially represent a variety of different metaphors. Led by the Holy Spirit, I would need to weigh the rest of the dream and look at every piece in context in order to understand what the snow represented in that instance. (We can use everyday occurrences like this to expand our metaphorical understanding and practice "seeing" symbolic meaning.)

Context is vital. We can't assume a word or element has the same meaning in every situation. Metaphors are *living* words. They are very contextual, and God can speak to us through them using multiple layers of meaning.

Suppose you had a dream involving fire. Fire could represent destruction or judgment, because when something is "on fire," it is often destroyed or damaged beyond repair. Yet fire is also used for purification purposes. It burns off dross. It refines. It can change molecular structure, such as turning sand into glass. So, when interpreting fire or any other element metaphorically, we have to be led by discernment.

That is why we cannot depend on a dream dictionary alone to interpret our dreams for us. In most cases, dream dictionaries present a generic, broad set of symbols and do not allow for living, active, and ever-changing forms of symbolism and metaphor, which are the result of God relating to each of us in ways that will resonate with our hearts. Yes, there can be consistent meanings with metaphors, but God is often speaking to us on more than one level at the same time. We have endeavored to create a dictionary that takes into account some of the many possible interpretations of each metaphor. It is available as a free resource online[1] and will continue to be expanded as time goes on. We invite you to peruse that dictionary, but again remind you not to depend too strongly on a dictionary interpretation.

One of the most impacting dreams I (Zach) had occurred a few years ago while I was still in the restaurant business. It was a very long dream, but to summarize, I was sitting in a sailboat on a massive sea. The dream's interpretation was that I could stay where I was, or the sailboat could take me to the other side of the sea — to Europe, where I later moved. Whenever I dream about sailboats, they often represent a geographic transition for me. Does a sailboat mean that for everyone? No, but it often represents that for me.

Again, it is very important that we do not assume that a symbol always means the same thing. Rather, we need to remain open to the Holy Spirit and the revelation He brings. In addition to biblical and cultural symbols, each of us has our own personal dream vocabulary that consists of metaphors that have special meaning for us individually.

---

1 *Visit our resources section at http://www.thedreamsbook.com/*

DISCERNING THE ATTRIBUTES IN A METAPHOR

How do we recognize what a symbol represents when it could potentially represent a number of different things? In most situations, God will give us clues to help us understand what He wants us to focus on within the context of the dream. We usually won't need to focus on every single thing a symbol *could* mean. Instead, the different elements in a dream will often contain particular attributes that help point us in the right direction. Those attributes will probably stand out to us the most or be highlighted in some way.

For instance, you could dream about riding a horse, and perhaps you kept noticing in the dream that the horse's gait was very smooth. Or suppose you had a dream about one of your friends, and what stood out to you the most was how extraordinarily kind the person was. Those elements are most likely noticeable to you because those are the attributes God wants you to focus on.

Important attributes may also be the ones that are out of the ordinary or out of their normal context. What stood out to you? What was strange, clearly missing, or out of place?

You now need to discern how to apply those attributes to the metaphor in context of the rest of the dream. If the horse had a surprisingly smooth gait, it could be that God wants you to know He is carrying you forward, and the journey will be smooth. If your friend was kind to you, depending on the rest of the dream, it could be that God wants you to know He is providing kind relationships for you.

The more we practice understanding symbols like this, the better we will get at it. We will start developing a metaphorical thought process that allows us to interpret metaphors accurately in the way the Holy Spirit wants us to in that moment with the dream He has given us. Whenever we see a picture — in a dream, during our quiet times with the Lord, or in Scripture — we will recognize that what we are seeing is potentially metaphorical in its attributes, and we need to understand those attributes in order to see the truth of what they are describing and then operate in cooperation with God.

This process of learning to recognize and interpret metaphors may be something that comes to you without effort, or you may find that you hit a number of roadblocks. The ease with which you "get it" will depend on the way you think, as we mentioned in Chapter One. If it is necessary for you to relearn how to think and process information, our hope is that you will find it somewhat simple as you go through this book.

The metaphoric interpretation flowchart is a visualization of a process that can happen almost intuitively. If we approach dreams with the process written out, as it is here, we can help ourselves avoid frustrating breakdowns and roadblocks.

The two primary phases are identifying meaning and applying in context to the dream.

We can have intuitive understanding based on the Bible and the personal, cultural, and natural functions of the object or action. It is important to remember that we can't assume the meaning of any symbol, but we can recognize that we have previous knowledge, and then with the Holy Spirit's guidance, we can

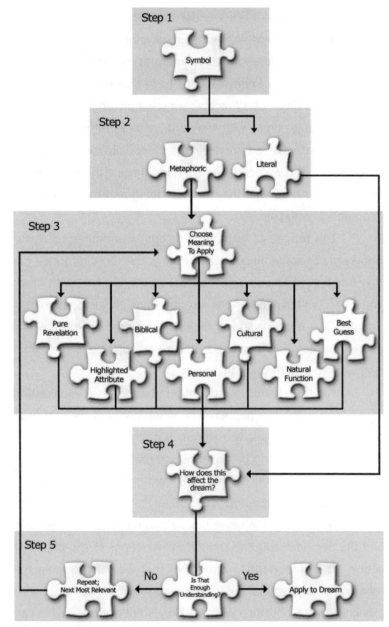

Figure 3.1 Metaphoric Interpretation Flowchart

"test" the object to see if that previous knowledge is correct in the context of the specific dream.

We must also leave room for direct revelation from God on the meaning of a symbol, or for the proverbial 'best guess'.

For symbols that seem to make no sense, it may require asking questions that can help us discern the correct meaning: Why this and not that? What is happening here? What would this mean if it were replaced with something else?

METAPHORIC INTERPRETATION FLOWCHART
(FIGURE 3.1):

Step 1: Identify the symbol to interpret.

Does this symbol seem significant? If it fits nicely with the background of the dream, it is likely not worth a great deal of attention. For example, if the dreamer was walking through a large forest, the forest is probably the important symbol, not each individual tree.

Step 2: Through discernment and context, decide if the element is primarily literal or metaphoric in its meaning.

Metaphoric symbols will often seem out of place, or they will be actively used but sometimes out of the context in which they are normally used. For example, if the dreamer is plowing a field with a dinner fork, the fork is out of context, and so you have to look at what it means in the context where you found it.

If the symbol is not out of place, it doesn't mean it is literal, but again, it makes it more likely that this is not an essential element that you need to interpret. To determine if you need to interpret an element metaphorically, ask yourself, Am I confused by why this is here in the dream? To determine if you need to use the literal meaning of an element in the larger interpretation, ask yourself, Does using the literal meaning of this element add to my understanding of the dream?

If it is literal, proceed to Step 4, if metaphoric proceed to Step 3.

Step 3: Choose which of the following metaphoric meanings to apply to your understanding of the symbol.

- Biblical Meaning: a symbol or a meaning found in the Bible. (Example: The number seven representing completion because of the seven days of creation.)
- Pure Revelation: something that God is clearly telling you at this moment. (Example: God might tell you after a dream what a specific symbol means.)
- Natural Function: understanding that is derived from the purpose of the element in the natural world. (Example: A hammer is used to drive something into place.)
- Personal Meaning: understanding that comes from your own personal history. (Example: I work as a carpenter; therefore for me personally lumber can represent my work.)

- Cultural Meaning: meaning that is derived from a culturally specific context of symbol. (Example: A four leaf clover in a dream could represent 'luck' in the Irish culture)
- Highlighted Attribute: aspect of the symbol that stands out in a unusual or exaggerated way. (Example: A really short giraffe.)
- Best Guess: a hard to explain impression of the meaning of the symbol. (Example: It is hard to say why, but I think the gorilla represents...)

Make note of the understanding in the area that you chose. It is always good to assume you may be right rather than know you are right. Symbols can have many possible interpretations. Move on to Step 4.

Step 4: How does your understanding of this meaning affect the interpretation of the dream?

Ask yourself the following questions about how the application of this meaning affects the dream:

- Does it change the dream?
- Does it reinforce existing meanings?
- Does it increase your understanding?
- What is the main affect it has on the dream?

Step 5: Do all the meanings you identified give enough insight to interpret the symbol in the dream?

Now that you have moved through Step 4, do you have an interpretation for the metaphor, and has this given your dream clarity? If yes, apply this interpretation and move on to other symbols in your dream.

If not, repeat Step 3 with other meanings.

In summary, Scripture has metaphorical content, and the Hebrew language itself is metaphorical. God speaks through the written Word, and He speaks to us in dreams. Therefore, in order to understand the language He often uses in both, we need to understand how to identify and interpret symbols, not just for their literal meanings but also for their metaphorical meanings. This is an essential part of what we are doing when we interpret dreams; we are opening them up to see what is inside them and making known the meanings of the symbols they contain.

CHAPTER 4

THE DREAM
CYCLE

O ne of the primary steps in continuing to receive dreams from God is showing Him that we value dreams. We know this is true from personal experience, but it is a principle found in Scripture as well. Jesus said in Luke 11:9 that what we search for, we will find. Therefore, if we study our dreams, God will begin to open them to us.

We can just about guarantee that every person dreams. You may not remember your dreams or be prepared to interpret them, but you *will* dream or have a dream. As we mentioned in Chapter One, a remarkable number of people who come across our path are certain they don't dream, but after they place their attention on dreams, they consistently come back to us with dreams they started having or are suddenly remembering from the past.

Adults may not remember their dreams because of certain spiritual or medical issues, stress, exhaustion, and rejecting dreams at a young age because they were scary. Our observation is that these issues, as well as the Western World's cultural attitude toward dreams, are the leading causes of "not dreaming." At this point, adults may have spent years training themselves not to remember or be involved with their dreams. Now when they wake up, they don't recall a single element or picture. Even though they are likely still having dreams, they would say they aren't because they don't remember.

Because this blockage usually begins in childhood, it is very important for us to value our children's dreams, to help them with what they don't understand, and to speak to them about the authority they have in Christ. The best way to show your children that you value their dreams is by helping them with the dream cycle articulated in this chapter. Apply it to their dreams just as you would apply it to your own.

The dream cycle we will discuss here is from the standpoint of the dreamer; it is the place you start from and the process you go through, from preparing to receive the dream to understanding the dream and bringing it to fruition, thus preparing yourself for another dream. Each of the steps included in this chapter is part of honoring the revelation God has given you.

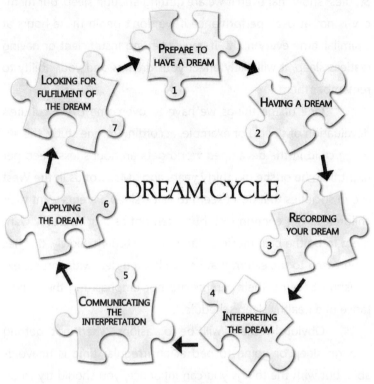

Figure 4.1 Dream Cycle

PREPARING TO HAVE A DREAM

This initial step may seem obvious, but if you aren't prepared to dream, you will have much more difficulty remembering your dreams.

First, you can prepare to have a dream by going to bed with the expectation of dreaming. Make a plan to get a sufficient amount of sleep every night, and go to bed at a regular time.

Studies[1] show that even if we are getting enough sleep, our memory is not at peak performance if we don't begin those hours at a similar time every night. If you're getting insufficient or having restless sleep, it will likely affect your dreams and your ability to remember them.

One of the things we have to overcome is the culture's devaluation of sleep. For example, according to one study, the average child in the developed world gets an hour's less sleep per night than he or she did thirty years ago.[2] Many of us in the West live in societies that don't seem to value sleep. Parents want their children to get enough rest, but often not as much as they want them to be the best musician, athlete, or student. Slowly, this has progressed to the extent that some children deal with chronic exhaustion because their parents are not emphasizing the importance of a healthy sleep schedule.

Obviously, there will be occasions when not getting enough sleep or going to bed at an irregular time is unavoidable, but with the things you can influence, you should try to do so to the degree you value your dreams — and your health, for that matter. When we combine this lack of value of sleep with the cultural belief that dreams are psychological in nature, it isn't hard to understand why many people aren't prepared for God to speak to them this way.

Second, your relationship with God greatly affects your sleep and your dreams. So, as instructed in Scripture, keep in an attitude of prayer (Colossians 4:2), being mindful of God, being

---

1 *Bronson and Merryman, Nurture Shock*
2 *Bronson and Merryman, Nurture Shock*

close to Him, and being in a place of repentance before Him. Going to bed angry (Ephesians 4:26) or living in an unrepentant state can negatively influence your dreams, particularly those God wants to give you.

Third, be prepared to record your dream. Have a pen readily available so that if you wake up in the middle of the night, you can write the dream down. We will be discussing this further, but this step in particular — recording your dreams — shows that you have a level of care for your dreams and desire to understand what God is saying to you through them. Not only that, but the *intent* to record your dreams can help you remember them. [3]

HAVING A DREAM

The second step in the dream cycle is actually having a dream. This step doesn't require a dream that is extensive, huge, dramatic, or necessarily meant to alter the course of your life. It can be a very simple dream.

You may not remember the entire dream; you may remember only bits and pieces or have just an impression of what was going on. But these are worth remembering and recording.

If you have not recalled dreams for many years, the sensation of having and remembering a dream can feel quite foreign. Don't despise small beginnings or fleeting feelings. These are the stepping stones to a much deeper and vivid dream life. It may take a few days, or even a couple of weeks — but if you press on, the

---

3   Visit http://www.thedreamsbook.com/ for more on electronic dream journals and other means of recording your dreams.

results will be, well, dreamy.

RECORDING YOUR DREAM

The third step in the dream cycle is recording your dream. As mentioned, this is a crucial part to developing an active and powerful dream life. There are many different tools available for this, such as notebooks and pens, digital voice recorders, reading lights, as well as the Stir the Water Mobile Dream Journal[4] but the important thing is to be active in the discipline of waking up and just getting the dream recorded. The key to recording dreams is finding what method works best for you.

INTERPRETING THE DREAM

If you have recorded your dream well, you have made the next step — interpreting the dream — much simpler. This step of the interpretive process includes preparing a rough interpretation (your "internal" interpretation that you use as a reference point) and a final interpretation (the polished, easy-to-understand interpretation that you could share with others).

This stage of the dream cycle is the first that isn't necessarily fulfilled by the dreamer. Perhaps you've had a dream that you've tried to interpret, but you just can't seem to understand what God is saying. When someone interprets your dream for you, he or she is stepping into your dream cycle and temporarily fulfill-

---

4 *Visit* http://www.thedreamsbook.com/ *from your web-enabled Smartphone device for more information.*

ing that role for you.

An outside perspective will sometimes make it easier to perceive the message of the dream. Many people we come across have dreams that contain really great and positive meanings, but they have trouble accepting these great things for themselves. This is another point where having outside input is very helpful.

COMMUNICATING THE INTERPRETATION

After interpreting your dream, the next step is communicating that interpretation. Communication involves having an understanding of the dream itself and being able to convey or record the interpretation in a way that fulfills the dream's purpose of positively impacting your life.

Many dreams are interpreted adequately but are not communicated well. We talked about Joseph, who communicated his dreams to his brothers but did it in a way that provoked them. Considering the circumstances, he may not have been able to avoid their negative reaction, but perhaps in most circumstances such reactions can be avoidable for us.

In this section of the dream cycle, we will be looking at the steps of communication, how different types of communication affect different people, and the importance of respecting the person or people you are addressing.

If you have interpreted someone else's dream, how you communicate that interpretation is vital. You want to give the dreamer a calm, collected, and succinct interpretation to the best of your ability, rather than an emotional, unfiltered, unclear, initial reaction to the dream.

APPLYING THE DREAM

Once you know the interpretation of your dream, the next question that arises is how you are going to apply the dream. There is no point in having a dream from God if you aren't going to act on it or let it affect you.

Applying a dream can happen in a few different ways. It does not always mean changing your immediate course or physically making something happen. When Abimelech was told he was going to die for taking Abraham's wife, he knew what he was supposed to do and set about doing it. That was a direct application. But with some dreams, this is not always possible. For instance, when Joseph dreamt about ruling over his brothers, God didn't intend for him to go out and try to make that happen on his own. Instead, in the long run, Joseph applied the dream by strengthening his relationship with God and being ready and prepared for when the appointed time came and God caused it to happen. With some dreams, the application means submitting to God in that area and waiting for Him to bring the dream about. The goal is to follow the Holy Spirit's leading and do whatever He wants you to do.

If you have had a number of dreams that clearly communicate what you should be doing but you haven't followed through with them, it clogs your spiritual "pipes." You aren't going to be as receptive to new dreams until you take care of the backlog. Be sure you act on the communicated, known will of God as it comes in dreams so that the *results* of the application can also be applied. Above and beyond whatever else that may mean, it includes the benefit of being in His will and being in a place spiritually and emotionally where you can hear Him even more.

God may repeat your dreams or repeat the issues they contain until you apply them. It is similar to turning on the television and finding the same reruns. You want a new season of the show, but you can't watch the new season until you have watched the old season. If you have a backlog of dreams, they have likely gone in two- to three-year cycles in which they were active for a season and then temporarily faded away due to the lack of response. If you have trouble remembering your dreams, it could be because you haven't acted on the ones you remember.

As you work through the process of applying your dream to life, it is wise to weigh the strength of the revelation with the cost of walking it out. Since dreams are just one of the many ways God communicates with us and they are often highly metaphorical in nature, in many cases, it is wise to look for additional confirmation when you sense that a dream is directing you to take a certain path. Some revelation needs one or more sources of confirmation. This can be particularly important when making big decisions. We will be discussing this in greater detail later in the book.

My dad (Zach) always used to say that you "hit what you are looking at." It is a baseball reference that means you can only hit the ball if you keep your eye on it. What you focus on — what you expend energy on — is going to have greater value to you. And things that have greater value are the things that you are going to notice. After I decided to buy an old Land Rover Defender

110, everywhere my wife and I went, I saw Defenders. It wasn't that there were suddenly more Defenders on the road, but I started noticing them because I had focused on them. If you are having the same or similar dreams over and over again, God is probably showing you that there is something you need to focus on and then apply in your life.

LOOKING FOR THE FULFILLMENT OF THE DREAM

After applying a dream, the next step is looking for its fulfillment. Until you see the dream fulfilled, or realize that it has already been fulfilled, you won't have complete resolution in your spirit. Obviously, this step of the dream cycle may take many years to come to pass. Even if you do all the previous steps well, you may have to wait for the outcome because of the nature of the dream. As a general rule, many "big" dreams will take time, prayer, and faithfulness to come to fruition. Big dreams are dreams that require a lot to change, a lot to come into place, or dramatic adjustments in life circumstances.

When God speaks to you, whether through a dream, vision, or prophetic word delivered by someone else, you need to be aware of the issue of timing. Just as you should weigh a prophecy and its long-term timing, you should weigh dream interpretations and their timing. Typically, most dreams seem to be for the immediate- to medium-range future. You will have some that are long term, but most will have a medium lead time in your life.

Watch actively. If you wait only a few days for the fulfillment and it doesn't come within that time, you may start to believe discouraging, unnecessary things about your interpretive abilities or miss your opportunity to watch the dream unfold later. This won't necessarily keep the dream from taking place, but by association, it may dampen your faith and hope.

If it seems that your dream should have been fulfilled in six months, but it takes six years instead, you can go back and see what you might have missed in the interpretation. This helps refine the interpretative process, as well as renew your gift and make you a better interpreter. It may also help you understand how you should apply other similar dreams.

REPEATING THE CYCLE

Dreams normally are not sequentially dependent to the point that you will stop dreaming if one dream has not been completed or applied; however, as more of your dreams complete the cycle, the more you will be able to remember them overall. This brings peace, hope, and anticipation to your heart. As each dream moves through the cycle, you are being prepared for the dreams that are coming, even while you are waiting for the fulfillment of others.

Again, one of the benefits of knowing these steps is that as you do them, you show God that you value the dreams He gives you and that you want to communicate with Him in this way. Even the simple things you do for Him in this area can greatly increase your dream life, your relationship with Him, and your knowledge of His ways and language.

Since we spend approximately a third of our lives asleep, it makes sense to use this time to help deepen our relationship with God.

> *For God may speak in one way, or in another,*
> *Yet man does not perceive it.*
> *In a dream, in a vision of the night,*
> *When deep sleep falls upon men,*
> *While slumbering on their beds,*
> *Then He opens the ears of men,*
> *And seals their instruction.*
> *In order to turn man [from his] deed,*
> *And conceal pride from man,*
> *He keeps back his soul from the Pit,*
> *And his life from perishing by the sword.*
> — Job 33:14–18

It is clear in this passage that God interacts with us for our benefit while we are deep asleep. We may not even be aware of it. So with that in mind, sleep *well*. It will profit, assist, bless, and grow you in ways that you could only dream of.

CHAPTER 5

REMEMBERING AND RECORDING

Dreams can be difficult to remember because they occur on a spiritual level, and we are trying to remember them in a physiological (or natural) environment. In a way, it is like trying to translate a conversation into multiple languages at the same time. Your brain may have difficulty remembering sequence, exact descriptions, certain scenes, and who said what.

Recording your dreams is the most important thing you can deliberately do in the dream cycle, because it is the one step you can influence the most. This gives it impact. When you record your dreams, you are showing God that you value them. Recording even that single glimpse or impression is still important. If you don't record your dreams, He may not help you remember them in the morning or later in the day because He knows you aren't planning on applying their meaning long term.

In a manner of speaking, recording your dreams is a spiritual discipline; it is subduing the flesh so that the spirit can prosper. Personally, we have discovered that the process of disciplining ourselves to wake up in the night and record our dreams has helped us develop perseverance in other spiritual disciplines as well. Additionally, God blesses us when we honor Him. If getting up to record your dream causes you to lose sleep, He is not unmindful of that; He will bless you and help you get the rest you need.

Do you have trouble remembering your dreams or believe that you don't dream at all? There are a few steps that could help you.

NURTURE PRAYER AND PEACE IN YOUR LIFE

One of the most important things we can do to help ourselves remember dreams is develop peace in our lives. Philippians 4:6–7 gives us a picture of what that can look like:

> Be anxious for nothing, but in everything by prayer and supplication with thanksgiving let your requests be made known to God. And the peace of God, which surpasses all comprehension, will guard your hearts and your minds in Christ Jesus.
> —Philippians 4:6–7

You can combat stress by developing a posture of trust and peace in your life. Cultivate your relationship with God and cast your concerns and cares upon Him (**Psalm 55:22; 1 Peter 5:7**). Ask the Holy Spirit to help you remember your dreams. Prayer and preparation tend to work wonders in all areas of life, and patience is essential to dream interpretation.

If you have urgencies in your life that are causing you to feel panic, fear, or pressed for time, your brain will shift your focus to those elements as soon as you wake up and let go of the peaceful dream you may have been having. If you are worried about something, your brain often puts memory markers on the issue so that you can continue to try to "fix" it the moment you wake up. A good dream from God doesn't always carry the same sense of urgency, so your brain may not automatically help you remember it.

DEVELOP A HEALTHY, ROUTINE SLEEP SCHEDULE

If you are not good at remembering your dreams, find out what in life makes it more conducive for you.

As often as possible, go to bed at a regular hour every night and get the proper amount of sleep. You may want to try getting up consistently every day at the same time, including the weekends. If you are getting up at six every weekday but at ten on the weekends, it could be affecting how well you remember your dreams. Studies have shown that "sleeping in" is not as beneficial as going to bed early.[1]

Hand in hand with this, try to find a way to allow yourself more time in the morning. Remembering your dreams could be as simple as giving yourself time to reflect on them as you wake

---

1 Bronson and Merryman, *Nurture Shock*

up. If you typically set your alarm for 6:15, wake up, jump in the shower, eat breakfast, and run out the door, you won't have time to write your dreams down, let alone reflect on them long enough to remember them. Your brain is so focused on getting to work or your other appointments on time that it won't be predisposed to remember anything.

Instead, try waking up before the alarm goes off. If you plan on waking up a few minutes early, you can lie in bed for those minutes and probably have enough peace to remember and write down your dream. Waking up and immediately having urgent issues to focus on will pressure you. It will cause the dream that is "sitting on you" to slip away.

We will be talking about different methods of recording your dreams in this chapter and later in the book as well, but being intentional about recording your dreams can also help you remember them. Buy a voice recorder. Pull the pen and notebook out of the dresser drawer and put them beside the bed. When your spirit has the *intent* of recording your dream, you will be more inclined to remember the dream.

As I (Zach) grew up, my parents made a point of valuing dreams, but during my teenage years, I had a full schedule, and I was more concerned with eking out every possible second of sleep than I was with valuing what went on while I was sleeping. This eventually changed — not because I had a great desire to see it change, but because my parents would ask me about my dreams virtually *every* morning on the way to school.

EXPERIMENT WITH YOUR SLEEP CYCLE

If the above steps aren't enough to help you remember your dreams, you may need to become aggressive by disrupting your sleep cycle.

In our natural biological cycle, there are certain hours when we are naturally more prone to remember our dreams. This stage of sleep is known as rapid eye movement (REM) sleep. If you research this at any length, you will find that there are nearly as many theories as there are studies about what is actually going on in the process, what the "source" of REM is, and what it does. But there is common agreement that this is the stage of sleep where we will dream the most deeply.

If you wake up during or immediately after REM sleep, you should be able to remember your dreams. However, sleeping straight through the night could "wipe the slate" and cause you not to remember anything. So discover in which part of your sleep cycle you are most likely to remember your dreams, and then experiment with getting up at that time. For some of you, if you don't get up at four in the morning, by six you won't remember that you dreamt at all. I (Jim) practiced getting up like this for a season. I set my alarm at different times of the night and discovered when I would best remember my dreams. I would get up, write them down, and then go back to sleep.

I (Zach) have also experimented with REM sleep. For a few nights, I recorded myself sleeping using the night mode on my camcorder. I then watched the video on fast forward and recorded how long I had been asleep before REM sleep started and how long it lasted. The findings were not totally conclusive, but they did raise new questions and encouraged me to develop a more regular sleep pattern. Having this information can help you understand when you should wake yourself up to record your dreams.

If you have children — particularly, if you have several children (plus a dog or two) — you learn after a while that getting up with them in the middle of the night doesn't have to be stressful because you will get to go back to sleep. The same is true with your dreams. Getting up to write them down doesn't have to be exhausting or even a chore, because you know you can go to sleep again afterward.

It may take some experimentation to find out what works for you, but it becomes a question of how desperate you are to remember your dreams. How much do you value the dreams you're getting from God?

Recently, I (Zach) was teaching on dreams in Switzerland, and a woman came up to me and said that she had been so desperate to hear from God about a certain matter that she actually woke herself up every fifteen minutes for two nights so that she could remember her dreams. On the third night, she had a dream that answered her question. God responds to the hunger of His people. He desires for us to draw ourselves to Him, and it is our actions that speak louder than words.

WHICH RECORDING METHOD WORKS FOR YOU?

If you were studying for a test or trying to remember how to do something that you haven't done in a long time, what would help you remember? Your natural pattern for remembering is very useful for dreams as well. You don't have to reinvent the wheel; use what you have used in the past. The Lord knows you, and He will work with you on this.

Once you've actively chosen to remember a dream, you will next need to find an effective method of recording it. There are three primary ways of recording dreams:

WRITTEN WORD

You can write your dream down using shorthand (short lines or words that will help you remember), longhand (writing down the whole dream like a story), or by making a list (writing down the key elements[2] of the dream, which allows you to put them in order later).

ELECTRONIC

You can speak your dream into a voice recorder, video camera, cell phone, net book, tablet, or other word processor. We encourage you to try the Stir the Water Online Dream Journal[3] as well.

ARTS OR VISUAL AID

You can record your dream by drawing pictures, making initial sketches as visual reminders, or by graphing it. For example, if you

---

2 *A key element is any element that is important to the dream and affects the main "plot."*
3 *Visit our Dreamer Resources (http://www.thedreamsbook.com/)*

dreamt that you and your friend Bill were at the mall, you could draw something to represent you, something to represent him, a line connecting the two, and then something to represent where you were. As you look over the dream later, this visual aid could help you remember what was going on.

We will be discussing each of these methods in greater detail in a later chapter. Depending on the way you process information, one or two of these methods may work better for you than others. Try each one, particularly if recording your dreams tends to be difficult. You will probably find that some recording methods are better for capturing certain aspects of dreams.

REMEMBERING A DREAM'S SEQUENCE

When you wake up in the middle of the night or in the early morning with a dream, you may not be able to think clearly enough to write it down in a legible, succinct manner. Pages of incoherent "Sanskrit" on our night tables are proof of this. It may be jumbled to the point that you need to draw the elements artistically or put them inside a graph, which could help you remember more of the dream or have some semblance of order.

When I (Jim) first started writing my dreams down, I couldn't remember sequence. It took me a few weeks of writing before my brain learned to keep track of the timeline of events. If you are having trouble with remembering sequence, it can help to record your dreams using an artistic format or by making a list. After doing this for a few weeks, you will probably be able to remember sequence better and start recording all your dreams in longhand or whatever method is the most comfortable for you.

It is not always necessary to write down your dreams in sequential narrative. In some ways, our memories are much more associative than sequential, so allowing things that go together to be written near each other on a piece of paper can help your brain recall sequence later, if necessary. For instance, perhaps the only elements you remember from last night's dream are a blue cow, some stars, and some jumping. Recording these elements, just as they are, will help you hold the essence of the dream and potentially remember the sequence later when your brain has had a chance to process it. Sometimes it can even be helpful to put "once upon a time" at the start of your dream and tell it as a story rather than trying to strictly record the dream just as it happened. You can always go back and edit it if you find you have gotten off track.

Many years ago, I (Zach) attended a summer camp in Tennessee. At this camp, we stayed in log cabins with bunk beds that were similar to what you would see in a submarine. During one of the evening worship meetings, my pastor and his wife prayed that I would receive clear revelation more frequently. They said this was part of my calling — to inspire revelation in the people around me. I remember thinking, *No one seems inspired.*

Over the next couple of days, I continued to contemplate their prayer and was uncertain what I needed to do. One thing I did know, however, as only a sixteen-year-old can: This word of encouragement must have been untrue because I didn't see it happening *right away.*

Later that week, I had a dream that was so impacting that I

decided to scale the bunk bed to get to my backpack so I could re-cord it. In doing so, I woke up most of the cabin, which, of course, led to questioning and eventually some good-natured ribbing. But the next morning, two of the other guys had dreams, and they woke up and recorded them as well.

Valuing your dreams and recording them will have an impact on your life and your relationship with God. As you grow in these things, they may also have an impact on those around you. You won't always be able to see that impact or influence in its fullness, but by valuing your dreams, you are building up within yourself a strong awareness of what God is doing, not only in your own life but in the areas you dream about as well: your family, your work, your church, and your friends.

That is our goal as followers of Jesus who dream — not simply to have spiritual experiences and divine messages but to be transformed by them and in turn, transform others.

CHAPTER 6

SUMMARY OF
THE INTERPRETIVE PROCESS

As we said earlier, there are many different methods for interpreting dreams. By sharing our framework with you, we don't mean to imply that it is the only correct method and that you have to interpret dreams exactly how we outline in this book. However, all good interpretations intentionally or unintentionally seem to contain consistent features. By defining the process, we mean to help you intentionally do the right things and avoid unintentionally doing the wrong things. If you aren't sure what you are doing as you interpret dreams, you won't know how to change, improve, or evaluate yourself. So by showing you our process, we want to give you a means in which to grow.

Having an articulated framework will also enable you to be a better learner. Even if other interpreters don't have the same "language" or way of explaining themselves, you will be able to distinguish what they are doing that works and more easily apply it to your own interpretive process.

The interpretive process contained in this book borrows language, terminology, and ideas from the Bible and prominent secular and Christian sources. Our intention in doing this is to create a framework in which you can compare your process to other processes and more effectively collaborate with other interpreters.

We will be summarizing the steps of our process in this chapter and covering each of them in greater detail as we go through the book.

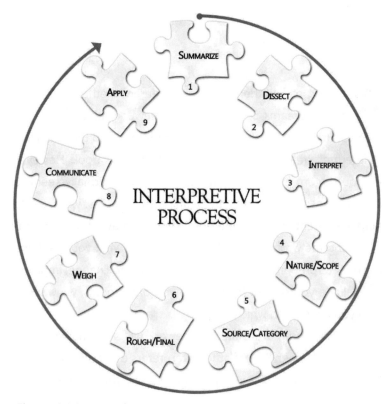

Figure 6.1 Interpretive Process

SUMMARIZING THE DREAM

After you have recorded your dream, the first step in the interpretive process is summarizing the dream. Dreams often have a lot of detail and "plot noise." If you can summarize the dream into a single core "story," you are identifying the important elements and preparing yourself to interpret the dream as a whole. You are including all major details but leaving out the "extra" material that doesn't immediately pertain to the main point.

When this is done well, you can sometimes take a ten-minute dream and tell it in thirty seconds, or a two-minute dream and tell it in ten seconds, and none of the pertinent details are left out.

If you dreamt about traveling through a city with your father, you wouldn't necessarily need to include every single thing you saw, heard, or talked about, especially if the dream was extensive. It could be that the point or core story of the dream centers around only two or three specific things you saw, heard, or talked about.

Supporting details or elements in a dream often repeat themselves and help define the dream's context. If you dreamt about your great aunt, and she was wearing a red dress with sequins, red shoes, a red belt, and a red hat, all of which you saw in great detail, you could summarize by saying, "Great Aunt Mary was wearing red." You often don't need to include every detail you saw; instead, you highlight what the dream seems to be emphasizing. This is a vital step in preparing to interpret a dream.

Finally, when you summarize a dream, give it a title. A

good title effectively allows you to do two things. First, it helps you remember the dream. When you read the title, you should be able to recall what the dream was about. The second purpose of titling is that it can further help you determine the most important aspects or elements of the dream. In fact, you will sometimes discover that a good title can inadvertently reveal the dream's interpretation.

DISSECTING THE DREAM

Think of this step as recognizing the different pieces of the dream and putting them in order. Here, you begin to pull the summarized dream apart and graph the different elements in order of importance.

The elements in a dream are the people, places, objects, events, actions, colors, numbers, etc. contained in the dream. Each of these has a different level of importance. The most important element is always the focus[1] (whom or what the dream is about); the other elements have varying degrees of importance following that. Don't skip this step because when you come across a dream that you don't understand, this step will often help you find a starting point. It will usually show you what to interpret first.

After dissecting a dream, you will have a list of elements of different types and importance that relate to each other through *context*. We will repeat this many times in the following chapters,

---

1 Holt, *Psychoanalysis and Contemporary Science; Hall, Jungian Dream Interpretation. Most of the terminology in this book (focus, dream element, key element, etc.) has been widely used since the work of Freud and Jung. We do not intend to recommend their works for dream interpretation. However, their common terminology can be helpful and the most comfortable to use.*

but context is vital. One of the most common mistakes in dream interpretation is assuming the meaning of a symbol by itself and not considering it in context.

INTERPRETING THE ELEMENTS

When you go to interpret the symbols or elements in a dream, start with the items that have the most weight: Begin with the focus. With each symbol, first determine if it is literal or metaphoric, and then interpret the metaphors. As you do this, it can be helpful to look back at how you dissected the dream and make certain the pieces of your interpretation are flowing correctly and in order.

If a dream is mainly metaphoric, there could be many different elements that need to be interpreted. Every symbol could have metaphoric meaning, and ideally, you should discern those meanings before you move forward and put together the overall interpretation of the dream.

Again, you are looking at the *summarized* dream. You aren't trying to interpret every single pebble, dot, and pen stroke the dream contains. You are interpreting the elements that stood out to you as having some level of importance.

In the 1950s, George Miller produced the hypothesis that the human brain could handle roughly seven pieces of information: seven numbers, seven items on a shopping list, etc. This was called the "magical number seven."[2] If you are trying to order more than seven objects in a dream, your mind will typically have

---

2 *Klingberg, The overflowing brain:* information overload and the limits of working memory

trouble keeping track of them, and thus things could be missed. Interpret only the elements that stood out to you as having some level of importance. Summarization can be a very important step, particularly with long dreams. If you are trying to look at more than seven elements, it becomes much more difficult to keep track of all of them in your head.

DETERMINING THE NATURE AND SCOPE

Regarding *nature*, dreams can be metaphoric or literal, while the *scope* of a dream determines the internal or external application.

After you have interpreted the individual elements of the dream, take a step back and look at them as a whole. Does the majority of the dream seem to be literal or metaphoric? Is it internal (about you and your life)? Or is it external (about others)? There is also a question regarding scale. External dreams could be about your office, church, or friends, or they could be about a city, a nation, or an entire nationality.

INTERNAL DREAM EXAMPLE:[3]

I dreamt that I was driving to work one afternoon, and over the radio, I heard someone talking to me pretty clearly. Using my name, they said that today was going to be a good day.

Explanation: This dream is internal because the dream is speaking directly to the dreamer. Dreams that repeatedly use the

---

3 *Some dreams in this book are written in first person, and other dreams have had the names changed.*

words *I, me, my,* and so forth are often internal. This is one of the things to watch for while trying to determine whether the dream is internal or external.

EXTERNAL DREAM EXAMPLE:

I dreamt that Nicole was walking, and she saw a train go by with the name of her employer on it. Each carriage had the name of a department on it. Some department carriages were really modern and clean, and others were old and dirty. The back carriage was labeled "the boss," and money was flying out the window at an incredible rate.

Explanation: This dream is external because the dreamer is observing events unfold that relate to others.

Determining the dream's nature will help you interpret the dream. For instance, if you know a dream is literal, it won't need much, if any, interpretation. If you know a dream is about you, your interpretation should reflect that.

FINDING THE SOURCE

Along with determining the dream's type, you can ascertain its source. Is the dream coming from inside of you — that is, is it something you are dealing with in your waking life that you seem to be processing in your sleep? Is the dream from God? Or is it coming from a negative source, such as the demonic realm or the negative spiritual atmosphere around you? Dreams could also be coming from a human source; most likely, this would be the dreamer's own mind, emotions, or desires. However, we can also affect one another's dreams; what is going on in others can affect what we see, feel, and experience in our sleep. The nature of this influence can be as varied and far ranging as the hearts and minds of humanity. Dreams could also be a mix of several different sources.

When you know where a dream is coming from, you will be able to interpret it more accurately and double-check that your interpretation is on track. Some dreams may have applications on multiple levels. For instance, you could have a dream that, on a personal level, helps you see how you are called to relate to people at work, but the dream could also have an external application in that it reveals to you the direction your company is headed.

Some dreams will contain aspects of more than one source. You could dream that a monster is chasing you through your house, but as you're trying to get away from it, you come across a beautiful, peaceful field where you know you will be safe. This dream starts with what appears to be a negative source promoting fear in your life, but in the second part of this dream, the source shifts, and the dream becomes one from God that brings peace and a sense of safety.

EXAMPLE OF A GOD-SOURCE DREAM:

Jade had a dream where a man dressed in white riding a white horse rode up to her and told her to climb up behind him. He put out a hand, and she grabbed it, climbing up behind him. She doesn't remember what happened after that.

Explanation: After waking, Jade realized this was a dream from God, one that invited her to follow Him more closely.

EXAMPLE OF A NEGATIVE-SOURCE DREAM:

Tony had a dream where it was night and kind of dark everywhere he went. As he walked around in a large, crowded room, he kept hearing people talk about him. Their backs were turned to him, and they kept saying how they didn't really like him and that they weren't going to tell him that so they could use him to get what they wanted.

Explanation: This dream really bothered Tony for days until he finally shared it with a friend, who explained that this was a demonically inspired dream given to him so that he wouldn't trust anybody. As Tony prayed that God would help him trust others, he felt peace, and the dream lost its hold.

EXAMPLE OF AN EXTERNAL HUMAN-SOURCE DREAM:

Samantha kept having the same dream every couple of days in late August and early September. She dreamt that she was the owner of an American football team, and in order to have a really good season, she had to pick available players from around the league to form a new team. She kept going back and forth over the same player, trying to decide if he would be as good this year as last year.

Explanation: After having this dream for weeks, Samantha

learned that her husband had joined a fantasy football league and was preparing to pick his fantasy players from the previous year's real-life league. As she realized the amount of thought and doubt he was putting into the task, she concluded it had been affecting her dreams.

CATEGORIZING THE DREAM[4]

This step helps you find the purpose of the dream (why you had it). Dreams coming from you on an internal level could be revealing your emotions or how you are responding to your circumstances. If the dream was from God, its purpose could be to give you direction, healing, warning, correction, encouragement, etc. If the dream was from the enemy, its purpose could be to frighten you, confuse you, or otherwise hinder you from doing what God wants you to do.

Dreams often belong to more than one category. A dream could begin in a negative or frightening way, for example, but it could end with God giving you victory over your fears.

THE ROUGH INTERPRETATION

Once you have summarized the dream, dissected it, put the elements in order, interpreted them, and now are beginning to figure out the category of the dream and what it means as a whole, the next step is crafting a first draft, or "rough" interpretation. This is

---

4 Vedfelt, *The Dimensions of Dreams: The Nature, Function, and Interpretation of Dreams*

an unedited version of the meaning of the dream. It gives you a starting point for putting together a clearer, more precise interpretation that you would feel comfortable potentially sharing with other people.

This rough interpretation is especially helpful if you are interpreting a dream for someone else, or if you are preparing to share one of your own dreams. It helps you get your thoughts in order and weigh word choice and the overall tone of the interpretation.

This interpretation should be succinct enough that you remember the dream when you read it.

PREPARING THE INTERPRETATION FOR COMMUNICATION

In this step, you take your rough interpretation and prepare it in such a way that others will be able to understand it. I (Zach) recently tried to give an interpretation via text message while I was in a hurry. The dreamer came back to me totally confused about the interpretation. In reviewing my text, I realized that I had failed to communicate clearly the full meaning of the dream. I understood what I was trying to say, but I did not communicate that. Instead, I communicated a version of mental notes on the dream. Your prepared interpretation should make the purpose of the dream prominent and clearly portray why the dream was given.

WEIGHING THE INTERPRETATION

As the Holy Spirit helps you knit the interpretation together, you should be able to feel a release in your spirit. You should begin to sense, *Yes, this is the interpretation of that dream.* There may even be times when you think, *Of course, the dream means that. It's so obvious now.* If you don't feel a release, the interpretation probably needs some work or simply time and prayerful meditation. As you grow in discernment, this feeling of release will become more noticeable and trustworthy.

Occasionally when you are interpreting someone else's dream, you may feel that your interpretation is right on track, but the dreamer disagrees with you. If this happens, it could be that the interpretation may need to be revisited or reworded, at the very least. However, it is not uncommon for dreamers (perhaps Christian dreamers especially) to feel that the dream means something specific and be closed to anything but confirmation of their opinion. It is up to you to discern if the dreamer simply doesn't like the interpretation or if it genuinely needs to be reworked. In any case, try to learn from the experience how you could have communicated more clearly.

Most often when you experience this, you will be able to recognize what is happening. For instance, the dreamer could have a dream about seeing a blue balloon and be convinced it means he or she is to buy a new blue car or marry the person with blue eyes. Sometimes the situation is not this clear, but it can be helpful to be aware of what the person wants to hear while you are preparing the interpretation. You might need to add a little aside about how the dream could be confusing and then tell the person what the dream actually means.

COMMUNICATING THE DREAM

Finally, as you go to communicate a dream interpretation, be sensitive to any language differences. For instance, if you are interpreting a child's dream, be sure to use words that are appropriate for his or her age level.

Also, be considerate of environment. Are you interpreting a dream for a church member or for someone you just met on the street? This can affect how you communicate with that person. Once while on an outreach in London, I (Zach) watched as one of the team members explained to a pleasant fifteen-year-old girl who was clearly seeking to appear very counter-cultural that the dream was saying she was covered in the "blood of the lamb."[5] Needless to say, that can sound really strange or even scary to someone outside Christian circles. We need to word things in such a way that the meaning is clear and understandable. Use language that is plain and easy to grasp.

APPLYING THE DREAM

When you know what God has spoken to you in a dream, the next step is applying His words to your life. With every dream application, the point is to follow the Holy Spirit's leading and do what-

---

5   *Referring to the power of the blood of Jesus, the lamb of God, for all believers (Luke 22:20)*

ever He wants you to do.

This concludes the summary of the dream interpretation process. When this process is taken from beginning to end and combined with a sensitivity to the Holy Spirit, you will find that the vast majority of the dreams you come across can be readily interpreted on an intermediary level. This means that after the dream is correctly interpreted, you will have a clear, working understanding of what God is saying to you through the dream.

CHAPTER 7

INTERPRETIVE PROCESS STEPS 1–3:
SUMMARIZING, DISSECTING, AND DIAGRAMMING

As we begin the in-depth discussion of our interpretive process, we want to bring you back to Scripture:

> *In the first year of Belshazzar, king of Babylon, Daniel saw a dream and visions of his head on his bed. Then he related the dream, giving the sum of the matters.*
> *— Daniel 7:1, LITV*

Much of the Book of Daniel was written in biblical Aramaic, which is in the same sub-grouping of languages as biblical Hebrew.[1] When Daniel recorded the "sum of the matters," the word *sum* is the Aramaic word *rash*.[2] It essentially means "the head of" or "the summary of." The pictures comprising the word are a head (representing the beginning or "head" of leadership) and teeth (understanding or processing something). So when considered together, *rash* means you are calculating or coming to understand the leading parts.

The word *matters* here is the Aramaic word *malin*,[3] which means a "mystery that has been ordered for speech." It is a group of words that you have to sort out and arrange in order to determine what is being said. Therefore, when Daniel recorded his dream, he was calculating the leading parts and putting the metaphors in some kind of weighted order. We know he did this because there is an obvious jump between the dreams Daniel recorded and the way he interpreted them. In the English translation of the verse, we don't see the process he used as he came to an understanding, but the word pictures of the original language show us what he did.

For instance, in Daniel 2, he related Nebuchadnezzar's dream:

> "You, O king, were looking and behold, there was
> a single great statue; that statue, which was large

---

1 *Johns, A Short Grammar of Biblical Aramaic*
2 *Strong's H7217*
3 *Strong's H4406*

and of extraordinary splendor, was standing in front of you, and its appearance was awesome. The head of that statue was made of fine gold, its breast and its arms of silver, its belly and its thighs of bronze, its legs of iron, its feet partly of iron and partly of clay. You continued looking until a stone was cut out without hands, and it struck the statue on its feet of iron and clay and crushed them. Then the iron, the clay, the bronze, the silver and the gold were crushed all at the same time and became like chaff from the summer threshing floors; and the wind carried them away so that not a trace of them was found But the stone that struck the statue became a great mountain and filled the whole earth.

"This was the dream; now we will tell its interpretation before the king."

— Daniel 2:31–36

But when he interpreted the dream, he hit the main points only:

"You, O king, are the king of kings, to whom the God of heaven has given the kingdom, the power, the strength and the glory; and wherever the sons of men *dwell, or the beasts of the field, or the birds of the sky, He has given them into your hand and has caused you to rule over them all. You are the head of gold.*

"After you there will arise another kingdom inferior to you, then another third kingdom of bronze, which will rule over all the earth.

"Then there will be a fourth kingdom as strong as iron; inasmuch as iron crushes and shatters all things, so, like iron that breaks in pieces, it will crush and break all these in pieces.

In that you saw the feet and toes, partly of potter's clay and partly of iron, it will be a divided kingdom; but it will have in it the toughness of iron, inasmuch as you saw the iron mixed with common clay.

As the toes of the feet were partly of iron and partly of pottery, so some of the kingdom will be strong and part of it will be brittle.

And in that you saw the iron mixed with common clay, they will combine with one another in the seed of men; but they will not adhere to one another, even as iron does not combine with pottery.

"In the days of those kings the God of heaven will set up a kingdom which will never be destroyed, and that kingdom will not be left for another people; it will crush and put an end to all these kingdoms, but it will itself endure forever. Inasmuch as you saw that a stone was cut out of the mountain without hands and that it crushed the iron, the bronze, the clay, the silver and the gold,

the great God has made known to the king what
will take place in the future; so the dream is true
and its interpretation is trustworthy."
Then King Nebuchadnezzar fell on his face and did
homage to Daniel, and gave orders to present to
him an offering and fragrant incense.
The king answered Daniel and said, "Surely your
God is a God of gods and a Lord of kings and a
revealer of mysteries, since you have been able to
reveal this mystery."
Then the king promoted Daniel and gave him
many great gifts, and he made him ruler over the
whole province of Babylon and chief prefect over
all the wise men of Babylon.
And Daniel made request of the king, and he ap-
pointed Shadrach, Meshach and Abed-nego over
the administration of the province of Babylon,
while Daniel was at the king's court.
— Daniel 2:37–49

This gives us a clue as to how Daniel interpreted dreams.
He was ordering the main facts, not simply summarizing the details. We can see that he did that; he didn't explain every little
piece. He explained the main elements.

In hindsight, it is generally understood among Christian
theologians that these kingdoms referenced in Daniel's interpretation are the Babylonians, Persians, Greeks, and Romans. The one
that will never end points to the coming of Jesus and the Kingdom

of God. You can find several commentaries on the subject for further information about Daniel's interpretation and how it is related to history.[4]

All metaphors in a dream have an order in relation to each other; they have differing weights and levels of importance. If you have a dream containing five different symbolic pictures, it isn't enough to know the meaning of each individual picture. You also have to know what the group means as a whole, with each element ordered to and potentially affected by the other elements. This forms the "sum" of the dream's meaning.

Daniel 7:1 is the foundation for the dream interpretive process in this book. We summarize the dream, dissect its parts, discover how the different elements relate to each other, and begin to see the dream as a whole. In this chapter, we will be going over the beginning steps of this process.

Before reading further, remember that none of this process works accurately without God's presence and guidance. We encourage you to consider these steps prayerfully and stay in a place of cooperation with God as you move forward.

STEP 1: SUMMARIZING THE DREAM

As you can read in Daniel 7:1, the first step in interpreting a dream is summarizing the dream. You visualize the "sum of the matters" and tell the dream as simply as possible, while keeping the plot intact. If the plot is significantly changed or seems to lack move-

---

4 For example, Daniel by Japheth ben Ali (ha-Levi) and David Samuel Margoliouth or Eerdmans Commentary on the Bible by James D. G. Dunn, John William Rogerson

ment after you have summarized it, you have probably cut out too much.

Summarization simplifies the dream and begins to prioritize its most important parts. Again, not everything has an equal level of importance. Take, for example, Da Vinci's *Mona Lisa*. It is a painting of a woman sitting down. Behind her is a great deal of activity: paths, trees, water, plants, things that look like they're dying, and things that look like they're coming to life.

If the painting were a dream, the dreamer would probably mention the woman first, and after that, he or she might try to describe all the different things happening behind her. However, the woman is the focus. She is the most important element in the picture. If you were to take her out of the painting, the painting would no longer communicate its purpose. That is how you determine the important elements of a dream. What is the subject, the key, or the most important part of the dream? What carries the most weight? Summarization helps you avoid being caught up in the details, and likewise, it also prevents you from ignoring the important ones.

After you have summarized a dream, give it a title. A good title helps you remember the dream and establish its main points. For instance, if you had a dream about a dog that was on a train, you could call your dream "The Dog on a Train." Just by looking at the title, you would have a grasp on two of the main points, as well as some of the plot.

A dream's summary may vary slightly depending on whether you are interpreting your own dream or someone else's, but the key is to note the essential points. As you assist other people with their dreams, the summary is also important because after they have communicated their dreams to you, you should be able to repeat them in a simplified fashion to ensure you heard them correctly. This practice will show the dreamers you were listening, and sometimes, it can also help spark their memories. The dreamers could begin to recall additional scenes they had forgotten that are crucial to understanding the dreams.

STEP 2: DISSECTING THE DREAM

The reason we summarize and remove the "fluff" from a dream is to bring focus and clarity. Yes, this means we are making decisions about what is and what isn't important to include, but we are taking into consideration the context of the dream as a whole and relying on the Holy Spirit to give us discernment.

The next step in the interpretive process is dissecting the summarized dream, which means pulling it apart and arranging each element in order of importance. There are three primary levels of priority within a dream: The focus is the most important, followed by the sub-focuses, then the contextual details and supporting elements.[5]

FOCUS

When Daniel recorded a dream, he calculated the leading parts and ordered the mystery in accordance with what held the most

---

5   These terms were popularized in the realm of dreams by Freud and Jung. It is possible that there were earlier sources who used them as well.

impact (Daniel 7:1).

The focus is the primary element in a dream. One way to help yourself determine the focus is by asking, *What do I mention the most when I repeat this dream?* It is difficult to tell a dream without mentioning the focus a lot.

Analyze the dream the way you would a piece of fiction or a movie. Removing the focus would be like telling the story of Robin Hood without mentioning Robin Hood. The protagonist is typically the focus of the story. Who is the protagonist in your dream? Whom or what does the dream center around? In a book or movie, we are usually the most concerned about the main character and whether he or she is going to succeed. This is true in a dream as well.

Suppose you had a dream in which you opened the door of your house, and your dog escaped and you started chasing it. But then you saw a different dog and started chasing that one. You ended up stopping at your friend's house and talking to your friend, and eventually you drove home. That seems like a fairly random dream, but there is a single element that ties the whole of the dream together: you. Different elements are involved, but you are in the whole dream, so you would be the focus, and the dream would be about you.

The focus of a dream not only carries most of the plot weight, but it has most of the emotional weight as well. If you had a dream that involved you and your brother, but for the entire dream, you were concerned about his welfare and it seemed like he could be in danger, the concern and emotional weight is on your brother. Even though both of you were in the dream, he is probably the focus. He is the center of the plot, as well as the center of the emotions and the consequence of the dream. If you were to remove him from the dream, the plot would no longer make sense.

Most of your dreams will be about you and your life. But you may go through seasons or have one or two dreams every so often in which something or someone else will be the focus. This could be affected by your life role or calling. If, for instance, you are a schoolteacher, you may dream about various students and ways you could help them fulfill their goals in life. If you are a pastor, you may dream about certain members of your congregation and the different struggles they are going through. So when you are trying to determine the focus of a dream, the important questions to ask are these: What *carries* the dream? What do you keep repeating as you relate the dream? What seems to bear the consequences and the emotional concern?

Finally, if you are trying to decide if a person or an object is the focus, all things being equal, the living, breathing element will usually be the focus, and the object will provide context. I (Zach) once had a dream about being in my car as it was sliding down an icy track with the parking brake on. The car was doing all the action, but the dream was about me. If the car had been a motorcycle instead, I would have remained the focus, but the context would have changed dramatically — and likely would have hurt a bit more.

If you follow these indicators, you will be able to find the focus. When in doubt, work through the dream using what you feel is correct. Often as you go through the diagramming phase of the interpretation, the correct focus will simply make the most sense. It is always possible to try the dream from a different angle if your first impression was incorrect.

SUB-FOCUSES

The sub-focuses aren't as important as the focus, but without them, the dream would be drastically different. Structurally they assist in holding the dream together.

For instance, in the dream about the dog that ran away, the dog is what caused you to leave your house; it could be a sub-focus. Sub-focuses may not be the exact center of the dream, but they will have a large emphasis in certain sections of the dream.

Initially, it could be difficult to tell the difference between what is important enough to be a sub-focus and what is just a contextual detail or a supporting element. It will take some skill and discernment to determine what has more weight and impact. At the beginning, this may feel a little arbitrary, but the more you do this, the better you will become at doing it well. Practice is necessary in dream interpretation just as it is necessary for anything we want to do with skill.

Ideally, you will have one or two sub-focuses in a dream unless it is a long, novel-length dream in which each scene is very detailed and separate. In that case, each scene could be diagrammed individually. If you are diligent in trying to pick out the sub-focuses from the other elements, you will become better at it. Even if you feel you are doing it very badly at first, your discernment will grow.

Discernment can be described as the ability to pick between two parallel categories. According to Hebrews 5:14, discernment comes by reason of use, which simply means that the more you do this, the better you will get at it.

CONTEXTUAL DETAILS
AND SUPPORTING ELEMENTS

After determining the focus and sub-focuses, you should distinguish the contextual details and supporting elements. These aren't highly significant to the structure of the dream's plot, but they help you decipher what the more important symbols could mean. Remember that we are still working with the *summary* of the dream; we are not including all the elements, just those that seem the most relevant to the dream's plot.

Certain elements will be in the dream simply because something needs to be there; they are more informational in nature (they fill in or provide "scenery"), and they may affect context or add nuance only slightly. In essence, they are filler or part of a transition of scene. If you dreamt about walking through your neighbor's yard and the grass was green, the color really isn't a contextual detail because most grass is green. It doesn't highlight the grass in any particular way or tell you something special about it. So when you go to interpret the different elements, you wouldn't need to include the color of the grass in the interpretation. However, if the grass stood taller than your head and was bright pink, those details would be out of the ordinary, and in a sense, they would demand some attention. This is part of the concept of comparing and contrasting. Things that stand out are likely to be more important than those that simply fit in.

In most cases, important elements tend to be nouns, and contextual details tend to be adjectives and certain actions that *color* or add detail to the existing elements, such as the color and height of the grass in the last example. Contextual details are things or facts that affect the meaning of the more important elements. If the grass is green, that doesn't add anything to the element, but if the grass is pink, that is unusual — that is a contextual detail that affects the meaning of the grass.

Emotions and moods often fall into this category. Strong emotions, either positive or negative, can affect the meaning of certain elements. If something makes you feel depressed, happy, or scared in a dream, this will help you understand what that element represents. Emotions in dreams typically won't be elements in and of themselves, but they can help you "see" what is going on.

For instance, if you dreamt that a huge cat was coming at you and you were too terrified to move, the cat probably represents something negative. But if you dreamt that the huge cat was coming at you, and you were happy because it wanted to play with you, that is probably a positive element. The elements are relatively the same, but they would be interpreted differently because of your emotional response to them.

EXAMPLE DREAM:

Jill had a dream one night where a cat that smelled of rotting meat kept scratching her hand every time she tried to catch it and then running and hiding in piles of haphazardly stacked boxes.

Explanation: The next day, Jill wasn't sure what the dream meant, but she knew the cat represented something that wasn't good, even though normally, she really liked cats.

KEEPING IT TO SEVEN ELEMENTS

After you summarize the dream, you should end up with about seven different elements, give or take a couple: the focus, two or three sub-focuses, and four or five key contextual details. Shorter dreams may have fewer elements, and longer dreams may have more. It may be tempting to include several more for a longer dream, but as an act of discipline, try to limit the number to *about* seven. Again, seven is a number that our memories easily manage. Supporting this concept, the Bible suggests that seven is the number of completion. (For more information about numbers, see Chapter Eight.).

If we can't "order" the dream like this, too much will be going on, and we won't be able to focus on the more important things the dream contains. Interpreting every single element in a dream requires a high level of mental aptitude. It is very hard to look at twenty-three elements and find an interpretation. But it is much more feasible to look at seven or five or nine elements and find an interpretation.

If you are a detail-oriented person, this could be difficult for you. You will probably want to include everything you saw, but if you do, you will have a much harder time distinguishing what is truly important in the dream. Once you have a clear interpretation, you can look at the additional details and add them back in. They should deepen your understanding of the dream and continue to fill out the context, but likely as not, they won't add any *new* core understanding, because you have already interpreted the important parts.

A good interpretation will make a hard dream look easy by focusing on the simple elements that are at the core of the dream.

STEP 3: DREAM DIAGRAMMING

One of the ways to help identify the elements is by diagramming the dream. It can make the interpretation process much easier. Diagramming is not a completely separate step from identifying the elements, but it is a helpful way to distinguish the different pieces, understand the relative weight they hold in the dream, prepare to interpret the dream, and maintain the integrity of the focus. There are several different methods of doing this, and you should employ whatever method is the most comfortable for you. The purpose of diagramming is to arrange the elements of the dream in such a way that you can see the interpretation more easily. You will often find that as you diagram a dream, certain elements that may have given you trouble before begin to fit together more clearly. So don't feel like you have to be rigid in this process — ease into it and see what happens.

Always start with the focus. That will help you establish the importance of everything else.

BUBBLE DIAGRAM

In a classic bubble diagram, you will always be looking at bubbles and lines. The bubbles represent the elements, and the lines show the connections between the elements.

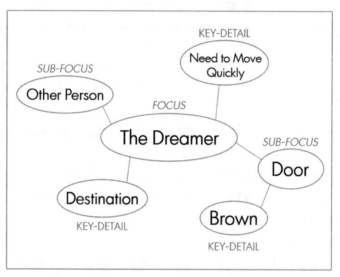

Figure 7.1 Bubble Diagram

EXAMPLE DREAM:

I dreamt that I was going out a brown door. Someone else was coming in at the same time, and I knew that I wanted to reach my destination faster than he did.

In this summarized dream, the dreamer is the focus, because he is the center of the plot. He is noticing what is happening around him, and he is trying to get to his destination.

To begin this diagram, you draw a shape in the middle for the focus. (For simplicity's sake, we chose a circle). Then you write "Dreamer" in the circle and mark it as the focus. If this were your own dream, you could write your name in the circle or simply "Me."

As you determine the sub-focuses, write them in other circles nearby and connect them to the focus. The door and the other person could be sub-focuses.

One of the contextual details could be that the door is brown. You draw that information in a circle that connects to the door node. Two other contextual details could be that the dreamer wants to move quickly and that he has a destination.

This gives you six different elements in this bubble diagram. Again, typically, you want to have around seven things, but the summary of this dream is rather short, and only six things seem relevant.

Once you have diagrammed the dream in the bubble format, it is easier to diagram it in other ways. Doing it a second time may not always be necessary, but if you are having trouble understanding a particular dream, diagramming it in different ways could help bring perspective.

LIST DIAGRAM AND SENTENCE DIAGRAM

The list diagram can be the easiest method of diagramming if you're helping with someone else's dream or if you wake up in the middle of the night and aren't coherent enough to record your dream using longhand. A simple list diagram lends itself to not having room or time to draw out a graph and also helps you have a list of elements ready and prepared as you go to interpret the dream later.

If you tend to think in a linear way, the list could also be the quickest way for you to diagram a dream. On the other hand, the list could be more difficult if you tend to think in abstracts. One of the benefits of the list diagram is that if you don't feel quite right about your interpretation, all the symbols are noted and written out so you can easily stick them in another diagram and see if this helps shed light on the interpretation.

FOCUS – Rats
SUB-FOCUS – Crumbs
SUB-FOCUS – Choir Area
KEY DETAIL – Excrement
KEY DETAIL – Hymnals
KEY DETAIL – Floor

Figure 7.2 List Diagram

EXAMPLE DREAM:

I dreamt there were rats among the seats where the church choir sits. They were eating crumbs on the floor and gnawing on the hymnals, and they were leaving droppings everywhere.

First we find the focus of this summarized dream. The

whole plot centers around the rats and what they are doing. If there were no rats in this dream, there would be nothing happening. So in this example, the rats would be the focus.

A sub-focus could be the crumbs; another could be the choir area. Some of the details could be the droppings, the hymnals, and maybe the floor. With the list method of diagramming, we simply write these things down.

Similar to the list diagram, the sentence diagram is also straightforward and often can be done on top of the original summarization. After writing down the summary, you can circle or underline what is what in the dream. You end up with the same list of symbols, but they are marked on the summary itself, so you can see the general plot of the dream and its highlighted elements at the same time. It can be helpful to use different colored pens as you highlight different elements within the summary. Or, if you are using a computer, you could type the dream and then highlight the different elements in different colors.

The sentence diagram is especially helpful if you have already written down your dream, or if someone hands you a written dream in need of interpretation.

Our Dream Interpretation Training Website[6] helps people learn and practice the interpretive process by using the sentence method of dream diagramming.

---

6 Visit http;//www.thedreamsbook.com/ for more information.

I dreamed that my good friend's wife had a snake that she could control. People thought it was cool, and she would bring it to parties and make it dance.

FOCUS - Friend's Wife
SUB-FOCUS - Snake
SUB-FOCUS - People
KEY DETAIL - Parties
KEY DETAIL - Making Snake Dance

Figure 7.3 List Diagram

EXAMPLE DREAM:

I dreamt that my good friend's wife had a snake that she could control. People thought it was cool, and she would bring it to parties and make it dance.

Again, we look for the focus first. In this summarized dream, the dreamer isn't in the dream, so the focus would be the friend's wife. The next important elements would be the sub-focuses (the snake and the people) and contextual details (the parties and making the snake dance). In all, there are about five elements here. Highlight them in the sentence and indicate what type of element they are.

ARTISTIC NODE DIAGRAM

This method is similar to the bubble diagram, but instead of drawing bubbles filled with text, you draw pictures that will remind you of what you saw in the dream. You don't have to be an excellent artist to use this method. The point is simply to record the images in a way that helps you "see" the dream.

In the dream about the friend's wife and the snake, you know the wife is the focus, so you can draw her and add the sub-focuses and the other elements. You then connect all the pictures as appropriate to show their relationship to one another, just as you did with the bubble diagram.

Figure 7.4 Artistic Node Diagram

EXAMPLE DREAM:

I was wandering the streets of a city looking for something. I didn't know what it was, but I kept seeing "To Let" signs.[7]

---

7   A British term for a space that is available for rent

With the artistic node diagram, you draw little stick figures of the various elements and then show how they connect. The most important part of this dream is the dreamer, so you draw a man who is walking. He is your focus. He seems to be in some sort of town, so you draw some buildings.

As he is walking, he is looking for something, but he doesn't know what it is. He is seeing a lot of "To Let" signs, so you draw those as the sub-focus. A contextual element would be whatever he is searching for; since you don't know what it is, you can draw something to remind you about it, such as a pair of binoculars.

You will often find more than one sub-focus in a dream, but depending on the length of the dream, there might be only one, as there is with this dream. Generally speaking, supporting actions are supporting elements rather than sub-focuses.

TREE DIAGRAM

The tree diagram, which is also called the sentence diagram depending on how you draw it, can be horizontally or vertically oriented. Both methods look similar to a genealogical tree.

This diagram helps you to prioritize the elements in a very clear way. As with a genealogical tree, the relative at the top is the most central figure. In this case, you are replacing that "oldest ancestor" with the focus. Each branch running off the focus and then off the sub-focuses is an element of slightly lesser importance.

With the previous dream, you know the sub-focus is the "To Let" signs and the supporting element is the searching.

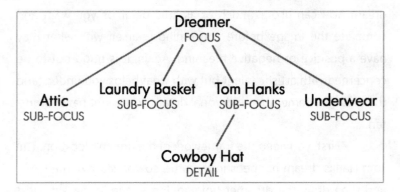

Figure 7.5 Tree Diagram

EXAMPLE DREAM:

I dreamt Tom Hanks was going through my attic looking for old underwear. He was wearing a cowboy hat, and I was in charge of holding his laundry basket for him.

In this summarized dream, the dreamer is the focus; the dream is taking place in his attic, and he is helping the activity. You have two sub-focuses: Tom Hanks and the underwear. The important details in the dream are the attic, the cowboy hat, and the laundry basket.

ARTISTIC DIAGRAM

The artistic diagram is helpful if you don't fully remember your dream and are stuck in the interpretive process. Drawing it out helps you to "see" the dream visually.

With the artistic diagram, you draw a single, still frame that gives you the best impression of what was going on in the dream. You can use as much or as little detail as you want and complete the image before concerning yourself with what may have a positive or negative meaning. Again, it is good not to be concerned with artistic talent but with what helps you understand the dream or remember additional details you might have forgotten.

First, you need the framework of the dream's location. The Tom Hanks dream happens in the attic, so you start with an attic and then draw the dreamer holding Tom's laundry basket. Next you can draw Tom Hanks standing there in a cowboy hat. He is looking for old underwear, so you can draw some in his hand, assuming that he's been successful in his search. Presumably, there are other items in the attic as well, so you can draw a few little boxes. This might help you remember other elements or something else that was going on.

The final step is going back and linking the different elements with arrows to help you remember or better understand the order of importance.

Figure 7.6 Artistic Diagram

EXAMPLE DREAM:

I am in my car parked in my parking space. I back up and hit something. I feel an impact, and then a man on a bicycle circles around my car. I think I hit him, but he doesn't act like he's been hit.

With the artistic diagram, you would draw this dream as a single picture. The dreamer is very involved in the dream, so she is the focus. Write an "F" and draw a little arrow beside it to mark the dreamer clearly.

Often while drawing out dreams, you will remember additional detail. Let's say that as you draw this out, you remember that the person on the bike is wearing a brilliant green shirt. So you draw that in.

The first sub-focus would be the action; the dreamer thinks she has hit something but isn't certain. This is a transitional point. It creates tension within the dream that is very important. The next most important sub-focus is the cyclist. From a contextual standpoint, the car, the bicycle, and the brilliant green shirt all have weight.

TARGET DIAGRAM

The target diagram allows you to pre-draw your graph. As the name suggests, the result should look like a target. The focus is at the center, and each layer denotes a different degree of importance. The more important the element, the closer it is to the center of the target.

This method of diagramming allows you to draw things out in an ever-expanding way, which helps you concentrate on the focus and what the other elements mean in relation to it. With certain diagramming methods, it is possible to lose sight of the focus or begin to forget the dream's purpose, but this method always keeps the focus at the center.

With the bicyclist dream, you already know the focus is the dreamer. The two sub-focuses are the impact and the cyclist. The important elements are the car, the bike, and the green shirt.

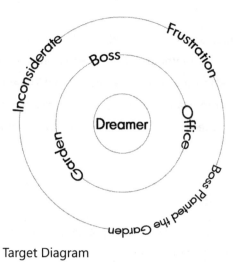

Figure 7.7 Target Diagram

EXAMPLE DREAM:

I dreamt my boss planted a garden in front of the office. It was filled with flowers and thorns, and I had to walk through the garden to get inside. I felt frustrated with my boss because he had made getting into the office so difficult. It seemed very inconsiderate to me.

In many dreams, you will find a limited amount of emotional influence, but in this dream, the context of the entire dream seems to be set around generally negative feelings. This gives you an idea of the meaning. If you were interpreting this dream for someone else, you wouldn't need to ask the dreamer how she feels about the dream. It is obvious in the dream itself. She feels frustrated and that her boss is inconsiderate. There is also a slight aura of intimidation (the flowers had thorns) that helps set the tone for the direction of the dream.

Keep in mind and be sensitive to what a dreamer feels in a dream. At the same time, however, not all dreams have strong emotional context, so you don't want to overemphasize it either.

With this dream, you can see that the dreamer is very involved in the plot, so she would be the focus. The three subfocuses would be the boss, the garden, and the office. From there, you can see that the details are the boss's planting of the garden and the dreamer's feelings of intimidation, frustration, and a sense that the boss is inconsiderate.

In summary The contextual details will help you see the context of the dream. For instance, if the dreamer were happy to face intimidation and difficulty, it would completely change the dream's context.

Interpreting the dream as a whole should be much easier if you do a good job diagramming and identifying the importance of each element. Should you hit a wall while you are interpreting the dream, it may be because you've given a symbol the wrong amount of importance or assumed something was the focus when it actually wasn't. If that happens, you may want to go back and re-dissect the dream, asking yourself, *Do I have these elements in the proper order? Is this element really that important?* Again, once it has been diagrammed correctly, the dream should be much easier to interpret.

The reason we diagram is that it makes the interpretative process less jumbled; the pieces are on display clearly. Diagramming helps us focus on identifying important elements, realize the relative weight of those elements, and lets us keep the weightier elements at the core of the interpretation.

CHAPTER 8

STEP 4:

INTERPRETING THE ELEMENTS
(METAPHORS AND OTHER DREAM CONTENT)

In many ways, dreams are like the parables Jesus told; they are allegories that contain hidden understanding. Jesus said that the disciples had the keys to unlocking them, but not everyone did. He often repeated that only those who had "ears to hear" could comprehend the deep truth of what He was saying. In other words, if God weren't giving them these keys to understand — that is, if they weren't waiting and listening for Him to unwrap the metaphor for them — then what was being presented wouldn't make sense to them. Jesus seemed to be suggesting that if they weren't *ready* to understand, they wouldn't be able to do so.

The Pharisees were slow to believe that Jesus is of God. Essentially, He replied, "If you are willing to do the will of God, you would know if I'm of God or not" (John 7:14–17). So at the forefront of understanding metaphors is the desire to know the truth. You are asking yourself, *What does this metaphor represent? What truth is hidden in this that could give me understanding?* You are looking to see the hidden meaning in what God is saying, no matter what that truth may be. It could impact you in wonderful, extraordinary ways, or, potentially, it could have implications you don't like. But if you are willing to receive, believe, and speak God's truth no matter what, you are prepared to know what a symbol means. Your biggest block to interpreting a dream could be an unwillingness to know and respond to the truth that God is communicating.

For example, some dreams will be corrective in nature. You could dream that you were handing black snakes to people or that you were holding on to a snake that you knew you should be killing instead. It is unlikely that the interpretation of either of these dreams is that God wants you to keep doing what you've been doing. As we have discussed previously, dreams slide past our initial defenses. They sidestep our arguments and go right to the source of the issue. If there is something negative that God wants to point out to you about yourself, He may do so in a dream. Dreams that are corrective in nature can be difficult to interpret, and you might have trouble being open to them and what God is saying simply because they are bringing potentially difficult areas to light.

The dream with the snakes is a very blatant example. In

many cases, "difficult" or corrective dreams are much more subtle. The point we make here is that if you have decided you don't want to know something, you have set yourself up not to know it. This does not always happen with the important parts of clearly remembered dreams, but it could happen with the details of faintly remembered dreams. Your mind could automatically erase part of the dream in order to divert you from a "negative" metaphor, and you may not remember the dream at all when you wake up in the morning. So again, in order to understand metaphors correctly, you have to start with the desire to know the truth.

CORRECTIVE DREAM EXAMPLE:

I dreamt that a church service was taking place. The presence of God was very strong during the worship. I watched myself climb up to the top of the roof and change into really bright and glistening clothing. I then tied a tightrope across the top of the room. It seemed really high. I then began to dance on top of the rope across the room. Soon everyone had stopped worshiping God and was talking about how holy and spiritual I was.

Explanation: In this dream, the dreamer is the focus. Looking at it in a broad, brush-stoke way, the dream is about the dreamer drawing attention away from God toward himself. It wouldn't be hard to think this is a good dream because of the strong presence of God, but it is a gentle correction dream that is showing the dreamer how his actions are affecting the people around him.

In this chapter, we will go over the general categories of symbols and what they often mean. It should be repeated as a precursor here that whenever we tell you that something means something, we are telling you that it *can* mean this, or that it *often* means this, but that meaning could change based on the context of the dream. For example, dreaming about a mouse in your attic would likely have a different meaning than dreaming about a mouse in your office or car. You could have the same metaphor in ten dreams, and in each dream, it could represent something different. This is why it is important to be in relationship with God and rely on His Holy Spirit while interpreting. With dreams, you can't assume anything. You can't take a metaphor you've encountered before and try to "plug it" into the new dream. God doesn't give multiple-choice dreams, where you can crack open a dream dictionary and pick meaning A, B, or C. The purpose of interpreting your dreams is to *engage* with Him. You are trying to communicate with God and understand the dream He has given you. Therefore, it cannot be handled formulaically. You have to search for truth and ask yourself, *What does this element mean at this moment in this particular dream?*

The potential meaning of a metaphor could come from a variety of sources. It is very good to go to the Bible first when you are looking to interpret symbols. In many cases, if the element appears in Scripture, it could have the same meaning, or one very similar, in your dream. Depending on the element, it could take a little time to find it in Scripture, but if you search for the answer and make use of your Bible, a Bible search engine, or your concordance, you will find many of the symbols you are looking for, often just below the surface.

For example, suppose you had a dream in which fifty of

your friends and relatives got together and decided they were going to start tithing. If you do a Bible search in the New King James Version for "fifty," the first verse that comes up is Genesis 6:15: "'This is how you shall make it: The length of the ark shall be three hundred cubits, its width fifty cubits, and its height thirty cubits.'"

You won't find this specific example in the New International Version or any other version that uses dynamic equivalents because they translate "fifty cubits" into feet or meters. So in this verse, we see that *fifty* is the width or breadth required to contain a new start. The ark was a new start for God's people, and its width was fifty cubits. So essentially, based on this reference, the number fifty is enough to contain a new start. Your dream could be showing you that God is going to start some sort of new and growing movement because there are enough people in your life who are willing to live with their finances dedicated to God. This is just one example of how you can find metaphorical understanding in certain versions and translations of Scripture that you may not find in other versions. Each biblical translation should state its interpretation principles in the beginning pages. We suggest a more literal version of the Bible when you are looking for biblical metaphors.

Metaphors will also come from personal or cultural understandings, clichés, and colloquialisms. On a personal level, if a certain smell or object always reminds you of your father, God might use that in a dream. On a more cultural level, many of the phrases and expressions we use in everyday conversation contain an element of spiritual truth, and God could use those phrases or expressions metaphorically in dreams. For instance, we sometimes say that an angry or frustrated person is "seeing red." Red can represent several things, but one of its common meanings is anger.

Whenever a metaphor doesn't seem to have a cultural, personal, or biblical meaning in a particular case, you may notice that some aspect of it stands out to you. God will highlight different attributes of the symbol to help you understand it.

You could dream about a lion, and in the dream, you are very aware that the lion is fierce or that it has sharp teeth. Or you could dream that you're in a car, and you are thinking in the dream that cars move quickly or that they have four wheels, and this is what makes them stable and steady. These attributes stood out to you, and they can help show you what the element represents in that dream.

Most symbols could mean a number of different things. Fish swim, but they also breathe water and have scales. Snow is often beautiful and pristine, but an avalanche can be destructive. In most situations, God doesn't want you to focus on *everything* the metaphor could mean; instead, there are usually certain *key* attributes that are emphasized in the dream.

One of the key points to discovering these attributes and interpreting the metaphors is, again, considering the context of the dream as a whole. It is good to look at the dream and ask yourself, *What does this symbol mean in relationship to all these other elements?* Compare it to what it would mean if it were a different metaphor — something similar and potentially *simpler.* For example, if you have a Lazy Boy-brand chair in a dream, you could compare that to a kitchen chair. Why is it a Lazy Boy and not just a chair? A kitchen chair is a place to rest, to sit, maybe to eat dinner, while a Lazy Boy is much more relaxing and more comfortable. If

God puts a Lazy Boy in your dream, knowing how it is different than a regular chair may help you come to a better understanding of the dream. A Lazy Boy chair could also be a word play that potentially means laziness or immaturity.

The positioning of the metaphor is also important. Is the Lazy Boy in the living room where you would typically find a chair like that, or is it up in the attic or flying through the air? What attributes of the element stand out to you or seem out of place? As you interpret dreams, you want to be sure you are answering the questions the dream inherently provokes. So if you dream that you're flying through the air on a purple Lazy Boy recliner, you need to address not just what the Lazy Boy means but also why it is purple and why it is flying through the air. These are natural curiosities provoked in the dream. They are the things you want to explore.

If you dreamt that you were writing something with a pencil, it is probably not out of the ordinary for you. It would be much more thought provoking to dream that you were writing with an ink quill dipped in liquid gold or a pen filled with glow-in-the-dark glitter. Why would you be using these things? Those are questions that almost have to be asked. The more a certain attribute stands out to you, the more *weight* it adds to the object and the more significant the context will be.

ROOT TYPES OF METAPHORS

Certain symbols that are similar in type and nature tend to have similar metaphorical meanings. We call these the root types of metaphors. They are grouped categories of symbols that tend to contain the root meaning of the base element.

For example, *buildings* are a root type; no matter what style or kind of building you dream about, it will typically represent what it contains. Your house contains your life, so a dream that takes place in your house would likely be about issues or happenings in your life. If you dream about the building you work in, the dream may have something to do with your occupation. Symbols[1] found within root types usually have comparable "root" meanings.

It is important to understand the root types of metaphors because once you know what specific symbols in these categories could mean in certain dreams, it gives you a foundation for knowing what they could mean in other dreams. If you know that *transportation* usually has something to do with where you're going, or what you are doing to get to where you are going (destiny, vocation, life purpose), you will feel comfortable interpreting dreams dealing with cars, trains, bicycles, and other modes of travel. When you come across different *objects* in dreams, in many cases you will be able to understand the basic core of the metaphor because you understand the primary function of that object. Interpreting the dream then becomes much simpler than it may have first seemed.

One of the most important things about the root types is that understanding them helps us realize that the Lord gives us the keys or answers we need to interpret what He tells us. He isn't standing far off and hoping that we will be fortunate enough to stumble upon the answer. Instead, He is actively revealing Himself,

---

1 *Dream elements that have a metaphorical meaning*

and as we study the root types, we will be drawn toward Him and His heart. So in addition to building your confidence in your interpretive ability, knowing the root types will also build your confidence in God and what He is saying to you.

Then, the more confident you are in Him, the less dependent you will feel on dream dictionaries to help you with your dreams. Over the years, we have observed that people who interpret dream symbols based on the context of the dream show much more growth in their interpretative ability than those who try to interpret dreams with a dream dictionary or a generic list of symbols. This is the kind way of saying that if you keep your dictionary handy, it will prevent you from growing, especially early in the process. Why is this? For one, metaphors are dependent on context, but additionally, the key to growth and learning is allowing an element of risk. You don't *need* to have a dictionary, because being familiar with the root types and dependent on the Holy Spirit will show you how to interpret your dreams.

If you become familiar with the following root types and not adhere to a dictionary for comfort's sake, you will show substantial growth because you are relying on the Spirit.

BUILDINGS

As we said at the beginning of the chapter, *buildings* are one category of root type. They tend to represent what they contain, whether that is your life, your church, or an organization.

Included in this root type, *rooms* tend to represent areas of life that correspond with the functional use of that room. For instance, a kitchen is where you prepare food, so in a dream, it could represent the preparation of spiritual food or the preparation of things that sustain others. Likewise, your living room could represent life issues, and your bathroom could represent cleansing or the removal of toxins from your system.

BUILDING DREAM EXAMPLE 1:

Camille had a dream where she walks into the office building that she works in, and the people she works with are there.

Explanation: The building could represent her job or her employing company because that is where business is conducted.

BUILDING DREAM EXAMPLE 2:

Joe dreamt about working in a post office where he is giving people mail that has a return address marked "God."

Explanation: The post office in a dream could represent the prophetic gifting because it involves bringing people messages (mail) from God.

BUILDING DREAM EXAMPLE 3:

Lauren has a dream where she keeps going to the bathroom and using the toilet and then very carefully washing her hands.

Explanation: A bathroom in this dream could represent a time or place of spiritual or emotional cleansing. In a bathroom, you get rid of toxins that are inside you (in the toilet) and wash off any contamination from the outside of you (in the sink, shower, or bathtub).

BUILDING DREAM EXAMPLE 4:

Bethany has a dream where she is in the basement of her school.

Explanation: A basement is the foundation for a building, so this might be about a foundational issue in Bethany's life. School is a place to acquire understanding, so this piece of her dream could be about an issue that is foundational to understanding for her.

BUILDING DREAM EXAMPLE 5:

Charles has a dream where he is in a colonial icehouse where lots of ice is stored.

Explanation: This could be about an issue in Charles' life that has been "on hold," or frozen, for a long time. The icehouse is where things are kept frozen until they are needed or until they are dealt with, and the colonial nature of the icehouse speaks of something that has been there awhile.

BUILDING DREAM EXAMPLE 6:

Miriam dreams that her mother has taken her to a beauty salon.

Explanation: The beauty salon could represent change in Miriam's identity since it is a place where people go to change how they look. That is, it is a change in how they view themselves and in how others view them.

TRANSPORTATION

In general, all modes of *transportation* take you from one place to another. They get you to your destination. So in dreams, they could represent the activities you're involved in, your occupation, or your calling, because these things are also taking you somewhere.

TRANSPORTATION DREAM EXAMPLE 1:

I dreamt I was in a sailboat on very calm seas. Oddly, my sail was up, but it seemed that the boat was not moving at all, even though the wind was blowing very hard.

Explanation: Sailboats are different from other boats in that they are powered primarily by the air rather than a propeller or oars. Because a common metaphor for the Holy Spirit is the wind, we could say that in this dream, the sailboat is Spirit-powered. So from this dream, it would seem that the dreamer is in a place where the Spirit is moving, but he seems to be unaffected by it.

TRANSPORTATION DREAM EXAMPLE 2:

Andrew dreamt he was on a train and his pastor was the conductor. He could see out the front of the train, and there was no track, but when he looked behind them, there was a track. It seemed like his train was laying the track, and many other trains were following him. Over to the side was a very old, rusty track with a couple of famous church leaders using an antique, hand-pump style of cart. They were shooting at Andrew's pastor and all of the other group leaders, trying to get them to come onto the old track.

Explanation: Trains are often big, very efficient, and tend to go on the track that is laid out for them. Since they are larger than a personal vehicle, they sometimes represent larger organizations, groups, corporations, larger social trends, etc. In this case, the dream is about a pastor who is leading his movement into new territory, but the older leaders who are on a different track are not happy about it.

TRANSPORTATION DREAM EXAMPLE 3:

Melvin dreamt he was on a really big motorcycle that didn't have a motor. Instead, it had ten-speed-style foot pedals. It was really hard for him to get it moving or to keep it going.

Explanation: While a train is big and carries many people, a motorcycle is small and generally carries only one or maybe two people. So it probably represents something very personal that relates directly to the dreamer. The style of motorcycle also matters. Is it a big, loud Harley Davidson or a small, quick dirt bike, and how is it being used? Why does it not have an engine? Why is it human powered? When you ask why-this-and-not-that questions, you will find your answer. The dreamer is doing something that looks cool, but he is doing it completely in his own power.

PEOPLE

Much of the metaphorical meaning of this root type is based on who the people are to you, what they have done in their lives, what their names mean, or their positions or roles — their inherent jobs.

A police officer has a role of authority in society, so in your dream, he or she may represent authority in your life, perhaps even God's authority. A nurse or doctor would potentially represent some type of healing or a call to be healed. When you understand what one type of person or position means, you will typically be able to figure out what others mean.

PEOPLE DREAM EXAMPLE 1:

Kirsten had a dream with an encouraging sports coach.

Explanation: A sports coach in a dream could represent a mentor in your life or even God himself. Both would be involved in edifying and encouraging you so that you function better in the roles you have. It could also represent a calling to be a mentor and help others in the same way the coach has helped you.

PEOPLE DREAM EXAMPLE 2:

P.J. dreamt he had a lawyer who was assigned to him in a legal dispute.

Explanation: The lawyer in the dream could represent someone who is an advocate for him. It could also represent religious legalism or a fruitless attempt to justify himself by prefect action as defined by a religious mindset.

PEOPLE DREAM EXAMPLE 3:

Pat dreamt she met a submarine captain and had a conversation she can't quite remember.

Explanation: A submarine captain could represent the invisible army of God or a hidden attack from the enemy. It could also represent a person with great authority who usually doesn't operate in a highly visible way. How do you know if the interpretation is positive or negative for a submarine captain or any other element? You use Holy Spirit-led discernment and the context of the dream. Again, as we said previously about discernment, you might not be very good at it initially, but you will get better with practice. Discernment comes by reason of use (Hebrews 5:14).

PEOPLE DREAM EXAMPLE 4:

Alfred has a dream where his mother is telling him to wash behind his ears.

Explanation: His mother in this dream could represent the Holy Spirit. In Genesis, the Spirit of God is described as brooding over the Earth, which is a very maternal action. Also the "washing behind the ears" could relate to the Holy Spirit's role in the New Testament of convicting us for potentially unknown sins.

PEOPLE DREAM EXAMPLE 5:

Sarah has a dream where her father is telling her how proud he is of the choices she is making in life.

Explanation: This could be God the Father showing up in

her dream in the form of her earthly father to give her divine encouragement.

PEOPLE DREAM EXAMPLE 6:

Hans has a dream where a man named Samuel talks to him on the phone and tells him that the purchases he has made are being shipped.

Explanation: Samuel is a Hebrew name that means "asked of God," so this could be an update on his prayer requests: They are being answered; what he has "asked of God" is being sent to him. Similarly, it could also be a prophetic message about God fulfilling his requests because Samuel was an Old Testament prophet.

ANIMALS

Animals or creatures in dreams often represent certain attributes of the animal or creature. For instance, a hippo is a large animal with a lot of weight that lives in or near the water. Dogs are "man's best friend." These attributes could give you clues as to what these animals represent in the dream.

Winged creatures often represent spiritual beings, both good and bad. A vulture, for instance, could represent a negative spirit, and a dove could represent the Holy Spirit or an angelic spirit. In addition, winged creatures could also represent people in your life. If you dream about a fragile bird in need of your nurturing, it could represent a fragile person who needs your care.

Predatory or parasitic creatures could represent demonic

or negative spirits that may be influencing you or others. They could also be an activity, a person, or some kind of spiritual influence. The creature's attributes, particularly the ones that are striking in the dream, will probably tell you what it represents. For example, a leech could be something that sucks the blood (the life) out of you.

ANIMAL DREAM EXAMPLE 1:

Tyler dreamt that he was walking down the street pushing a baby stroller. As he walked past the home he grew up in, he noticed several scary snakes that were approaching his child.

Explanation: We can assume that the snakes are negative since the dreamer is scared of them. This dream seems to be about lies in Tyler's past that are now threatening his child. Snakes are associated with deception based on the biblical precedent in Genesis in the Garden of Eden.

ANIMAL DREAM EXAMPLE 2:

Elizabeth dreamt that she and her husband were in some kind of compound/camp. There were lots of people and animals around, particularly horses. There was a horrible great white shark being kept locked up in one of the horseboxes out of the water. It broke free and somehow came chasing after her and her husband. It cornered them and was about to strike when a beautiful white horse got in the way. The shark got it instead, and they managed to escape.

Explanation: A shark in a horsebox is a shark that is out of place. A horsebox is, obviously, a place for horses. Horses often represent power or influence since they are powerful animals and historically have been ridden by people with influence. So a shark in a horsebox is a social predator that has taken a place of influence. This is not a very happy dream, but it could be a very timely warning.

ANIMAL DREAM EXAMPLE 3:

Samantha dreamt she was a red squirrel running around picking up coins from a field. She carried them all back to her hole and started over.

Explanation: Red squirrels are very productive but sometimes frantic hoarders. Samantha is working very hard to earn money but may have lost her perspective.

OBJECTS

Objects in dreams tend to represent their function, something related to their purpose, or the cultural value given to them. Weapons, for example, are used to cause harm, to defend, or to attack, and they can also represent words or actions, which have similar purposes.

Workout equipment is another good example of how an object's function will reveal its meaning. In "real life," you know that the general purpose of workout equipment is to strengthen the body, so if you dream about being at the gym, you could look at the context of your dream and ask yourself, *What is it that I'm strengthening or that God is strengthening within me? What is it I'm working on?* This can help you understand what God may be telling you to improve or address.

Clothing often relates to how you are prepared or equipped to deal with certain environments and actives. Culture and vocation are two common contexts that affect the meaning of clothes. Wearing farmers' clothing while running a marathon would give you a much different meaning than wearing only a baseball cap.

Parts and pieces of objects can have meaning based on how they function and fit into the larger object. This includes body parts. Your legs can represent your spiritual walk because they help the body walk. Your head can represent leadership because it leads the body.

Sometimes the five fingers of the hand map to the five-fold gifts in Ephesians 4: the thumb representing the apostolic because it touches all the other gifts; the pointer representing the prophetic because it points the way; the middle finger representing evangelism because it has the greatest reach; the ring finger representing the pastoral call to the Church, Christ's bride; and the pinky finger mapped to the teacher's call to teach things in small, manageable ways.

Food is another important type of object, ranging from the biblical examples of milk and meat (1 Corinthians 3:1–3) to cultural and personal contexts.

OBJECT DREAM EXAMPLE 1:

Jane had a dream about a Christmas present that had a pencil inside.

Explanation: Because it is a writing instrument, a pencil could represent a calling or a gift from God to write in some fashion. (A typewriter or word processor could represent something similar.) A pencil could also represent an action that is correctable because you can erase what you write. A permanent marker would not represent this same correctable nature.

OBJECT DREAM EXAMPLE 2:

Betty has a dream where she is holding a tube of glue. Everywhere she goes, she is holding the same tube.

Explanation: Glue could represent a calling or an ability to "bond" with others. It could also represent an ability to fix broken situations by putting them back together. Conversely, it could represent a superficial attempt to repair an unfixable situation.

OBJECT DREAM EXAMPLE 3:

Max dreams he is using gardening clippers to give people haircuts.

Explanation: This could represent the need to prune something that is starting to grow out of control or needs correction. Depending on the context, Max could be the target or the vehicle of the pruning.

OBJECT DREAM EXAMPLE 4:

Cassandra has a dream where she is polishing a trophy in her room.

Explanation: A trophy is usually given in honor of some act. Alternatively, it could represent pride because we often have pride in our own honored achievements.

OBJECT DREAM EXAMPLE 5:

Logan has a dream where he and his neighbor are shooting at each other with handguns.

Explanation: Handguns are for personal use and obviously can be painful. The handguns in this dream could represent hurtful words spoken in a personal way. Bullets move through the air just as words do.

OBJECT DREAM EXAMPLE 6:

Ruby has a dream where she is eating a lime out of the pile in front of her.

Explanation: The limes could represent some sour things she needs to process, but it will be good for her if she does. Limes are sour, but they are healthy fruit that have a lot of vitamin C and other nutrients.

OBJECT DREAM EXAMPLE 7:

Corey has a dream where he is in front of an oven that has very hot pans of fresh bread inside. In the dream, Corey is wearing oven mitts.

Explanation: The bread represents the fresh words of God, but the pans are hot, which means that they have to be handled with care. The oven mitts show that Corey is equipped to carefully handle the fresh words of God.

OBJECT DREAM EXAMPLE 8:

Ryan has a dream where his pointer finger keeps on getting injured in strange accidents.

Explanation: The pointer finger can represent the prophetic gifting because it points out direction, or it could simply represent direction.

ACTIONS AND CONDITIONS

When you look at different *actions and conditions* in a dream, you first want to look at what would be natural to you and then at what is enhanced or different. What breaks the traditional rules of physics and so on?

For instance, many people have dreams in which they can fly. This activity is evocative of moving through space and sky, of being completely free of traditional gravity, so it often represents moving in different ways or levels in the Spirit. This is not normal behavior for humans in the natural, so it stands out in a dream.

Another common example found in this root type is running in slow motion. This tends to happen in nightmares or other frightening dreams where the dreamer is trying to get away from something. As that is the case, running in slow motion can represent being ruled by fear. The dream may be showing you that your efforts to escape the issue are ineffectual, implying that you should take a different approach.

In a similar way, free falling in a dream could represent insecurity or not being grounded.

Direction can be considered a condition of orientation. It could have meaning based on the points of the compass. The sun rises in the east, so east might represent a beginning. Likewise, west is the direction of the sunset and could represent the ending of a cycle. Right could be mapped to the dominant hand for most people and could represent what you are able to do especially "right" now. Left, usually being the non-dominant hand, could represent something you are holding on to for the future or an undeveloped potential.

Again, by examining certain metaphors in certain dreams, you can more easily see how similar symbols could have similar meanings in other dreams.

ACTIONS AND CONDITIONS DREAM EXAMPLE 1:

Dana has a dream where she is diving into the deep end of a pool.

Explanation: Diving into water could represent going deep into things of the Holy Spirit or going off the "deep end" into more than you can handle. In the first case, water would represent things of the Spirit, and in the second case, it would represent issues or troubles.

ACTIONS AND CONDITIONS DREAM EXAMPLE 2:

Dennis has a dream about going fishing.

Explanation: In line with Jesus' use of the metaphor in Mark 1:7, fishing could represent evangelism in that you are catching people (the fish) and moving them from living in the realm below to living in the realm above. In contrast, fishing could also represent a grasping for ideas, solutions, or the truth (blindly groping for things under the surface to see what you will catch). It is also an old pastime and may be relaxing.

ACTIONS AND CONDITIONS DREAM EXAMPLE 3:

Sherry has a dream where she is continuously sprinting everywhere she goes.

Explanation: Sprinting in a positive context could indicate advancing rapidly in some area of spiritual growth or success. In a negative context, it could represent fleeing a situation with great haste or panic.

WEATHER SYSTEMS AND GEOLOGICAL EVENTS

Another root type is *weather systems and geological events*. Some of these are occasionally referred to as acts of God. In order to know what a storm, an earthquake, or some other natural phenomenon would represent, you first have to ascertain its source. To do this, it is good to look at the coloration of the storm in the dream (dark or light) and the implied *intent* of the storm or natural phenomenon. Tsunamis and hurricanes tend to be devastating in the natural, but in a dream they could represent a cleansing of the land. Alternatively, you could have a similar storm or element coming with a destructive intent: A tornado could be coming to destroy your house. That could represent an attack. So you have to look at the symbol in context.

GEOLOGICAL EVENTS DREAM EXAMPLE:

Johnny dreamt that he was driving a pickup truck through a flood of dirty water. The water was just over his tires, and he couldn't see anything but water for miles.

Explanation: As with many dreams, this could be predictive or prophetic of a literal event. From a metaphorical standpoint, it could also represent a situation that changes in a dramatic or sudden way.

WEATHER SYSTEMS DREAM EXAMPLE 1:

Hannah dreamt she was climbing a tree when suddenly, out of a clear blue sky, a tornado came and picked her up and carried her for miles and miles until she could see the whole earth almost like a globe. Her attention was drawn very strongly to England and Wales. It was like they were glowing with honey.

Explanation: This tornado appears to be a "friendly" tornado, giving the dreamer a fresh perspective. The dream is pulling her out of her present situation and showing her something very interesting. It is not clear in this dream why she is being shown England and Wales, but some options are prayer, missions, move, support, etc.

WEATHER SYSTEMS DREAM EXAMPLE 2:

Douglas had a dream that he was on his motorbike going as fast as it would go (really, really fast). But he was being chased by a large dark cloud that sort of resembled someone he knew, like some sort of monster that you might see in a *Lord of the Rings*-type movie. He felt like the cloud wanted to own him or kill him.

Explanation: Clouds are things that influence the environment. They also can be found at many altitudes, metaphorically implying Second or Third Heaven activity. This dream is showing Douglas the intent of the enemy or some other type of dark spiritual influence. With this dream, the best thing to do would be to take a stand and reject the fear and authority that the being represents.

Those are the seven basic root types of metaphors: buildings, transportation, people, animals, objects, actions and conditions, and weather systems. If you can learn these seven types, they will help you understand a host of symbols in dreams. In many instances, the meaning of the individual metaphors in these categories is a variation or specification of the general meaning of the root type.

SELF-REFERENCING SYMBOL CATEGORIES

Symbols found in the *self-referencing symbol categories* have independent meanings that are not necessarily related to similar symbols. For example, the meaning of one color can be completely unrelated to the meaning of another color (unless they are very similar colors, such as two different shades of blue). Red and blue have very different meanings; black has a very different meaning than white, and so on.

How is this different than symbols found within the root types? All buildings, no matter the style or purpose, will usually have a related meaning. Colors, on the other hand, have a wide range of meanings that are unrelated to one another.

COLORS

Colors tend to affect context; they can "shade" what everything else means and can add particular meaning to something that is specifically colored. A brightly colored building, for instance, may still represent your life or your organization, but the color will tell you very contextual things about it.

Novice dream interpreters sometimes get so excited about seeing colors that they will take a color, make it a noun instead of an adjective, and end up losing whatever that color is supposed to represent. Typically, colors are not the "main attraction" of a dream. They are modifiers. Returning to an earlier reference, if you dream that the grass is pink, the odd color will make the grass stand out and let you know that you should be paying attention to something — not the pink in and of itself but the grass and why it is that color. The pink shows you something specific about the grass, but it doesn't override the grass.

Colors in a dream can help show a symbol's importance, nature, or quality. They cause you to ask a question: *Why is the grass pink instead of green?* A particular symbol may not seem all that important in the infrastructure of a dream, but when it is highlighted with a peculiar color, it could carry greater weight.

The vibrancy of the color can also tell you things about the symbol. Brilliant, glowing color in your dream could mean bright things of the Spirit, while objects or places that are dull or dark could represent things that are not "of the light" or hidden in some way. Similarly, if there is no color in a dream — it is black and white or shades of brown — you could be dealing with "darker" subject matter, something the light of God isn't penetrating. Or the dream could be coming from a source that has no inherent light in it, such as the enemy or the dark recesses of your insecurity or fear. It could also be a dream in which color has no role and so is not memorable.

The question to ask with colors is this: *What is my attention drawn to?* If a color doesn't stand out in a particular way, it could be a neutral element: something that is there because something needs to be there. If you're wearing a blue t-shirt in a dream and you always wear blue, the blue probably is not that important. But if you never wear blue t-shirts and you're wearing one in a dream, it could be a little more significant. What stands out as unexpected? That is what you are looking for.

The meanings of colors come from a variety of places. You are probably familiar with some of the social or colloquial understandings of color. For example, you may have grown up hearing expressions such as "green with envy," "feeling blue," or "seeing red," as we mentioned. In most cases, these associations are in place because there is some spiritual truth within them.

We also look at the physics of color: how it functions and the biology of how we process it. Everything that has been proven in physics was created by God to work that way, so truths in science help reveal His intended purpose for color.

And, of course, the foundation to which we always return for validity is precedence and use in Scripture, as well as the root meaning of the symbols in ancient Hebrew.

Colors are used throughout Scripture in precise ways, and every time a color is mentioned, it helps us see the purpose God has for that color. For instance, He created the rainbow for a specific time, a specific place, and a specific reason. This helps us understand what the rainbow is as a whole and how we should treat it.

There seems to be in Scripture a general understanding that the rainbow, this display of color, represents the Spirit of God. We see this in Revelation 4, which talks about the rainbow depicting His Spirit around the throne. We see this also in Genesis after the flood, when God used it to reveal His Spirit and His promise. Only God can remind Himself not to do something, because no one else has any credibility to do that. So when He placed the rainbow in the sky, He was reminding us of His promise, and He was also reminding Himself by Himself never to destroy the Earth with water again (Genesis 9:13, 16).

From a physics standpoint, we understand that white light is actually composed of multiple colors of light. When we diffract white light through a prism (thus "bending" the light), it will display different colors. That is essentially what happens in the atmosphere when we see a rainbow. White light enters through water particles at an angle and displays its different spectrums — seven of them, when the original white light is included.

According to multiple references in Revelation, the Spirit of God is a sevenfold Spirit. In Isaiah 11:2, those seven Spirits are mentioned by name. When we align the colors of the rainbow with the seven Spirits named in Isaiah 11:2, we begin to see some amazing correlations not just with the meanings of colors, but also with the nature of God and His ways:

> *The Spirit of the LORD will rest on Him, The spirit of wisdom and understanding, The spirit of counsel and strength, The spirit of knowledge and the fear of the LORD.*
> — Isaiah 11:2

Returning to physics, different colors have different wavelengths. If we take the seven colors of the rainbow and the sevenfold Spirit of God and consider them together in their respective sequence, we have the whole Spirit being white. White light, when diffracted, displays wisdom as red, understanding as orange, counsel as yellow, strength as green, and knowledge as blue. Indigo and violet are part of the mnemonic of ROY-G-BIV (how the colors are often taught in science), so when considered together, they are the color purple, which corresponds to the last attribute mentioned in Isaiah 11:2, which is the fear of the Lord.

This gives us great depth of insight into the nature and

purpose of color. For instance, purple has the smallest wavelengths and is at the top of the rainbow, aligning with the Spirit of the Fear of the Lord. According to physics, tighter wavelengths such as purple are the most powerful because they have the most energy; there are many more waves in a smaller space. This implies that the Spirit of the Fear of the Lord is very, very powerful and steadfast.

At the same time, the smaller the wavelength, the easier it is for that color of light to diffract. Just as it is easy for purple light to be diffracted from white, it is very easy for God's people to lose their fear of the Lord.[2]

Just as purple light is easy to diffract, red light is the most difficult to diffract, because it has the longest wavelength. Red is wisdom, and unlike the fear of the Lord, wisdom is difficult to lose, because when we are truly wise, we are in tune with the ways of God.

Using another metaphor to help explain this metaphor, it is similar to the tires on a car. When a car with large tires (longer wavelengths) comes in contact with a bump in the road, it doesn't affect the car nearly as much as it would if the car had small tires (smaller wavelengths). It is easy to lose track of the fear of the Lord, but it is difficult to lose wisdom.

Scripture contains many other insights into color. Again, every time color is mentioned, God is revealing a specific purpose contained within that color, and the context in which it appears will often help us recognize what that purpose is.

---

2 For more information on the fear of the Lord, we recommend The 7 Spirits of God by Jim Driscoll, available on www.stirthewater.com

For example, God prescribed colors for the Tabernacle in the Old Testament. Everything in the Holy of Holies was to be made of gold. Gold must first be purified, but once it is, it is *very* pure; it is costly and expensive. Gold often represents the glory of God. Bronze, a substance that is tempered in fire and very strong, was used for the altar. Ezekiel talks about lapis lazuli, the brilliant blue color of the throne. These are but a few examples; Scripture contains many more.

COLOR DREAM EXAMPLE 1:

Rick had a dream where he lived in a house that had been painted green inside and out. Every room he went into was green.

Explanation: Green in a dream might represent growth because plants that are growing and thriving tend to be that color. Green could also represent jealousy (using the culture clue of being "green with envy"). Also, green could represent the Spirit of might and victory (based on aligning the seven colors associated with the rainbow with the sevenfold Spirit of God enumerated in Isaiah 11:2). In bringing the first and last together, people who are operating in the Spirit of might and victory tend to grow.

COLOR DREAM EXAMPLE 2:

David dreams that he opens his dresser drawer, and all his clothes are shades of brown.

Explanation: Brown in a dream could represent humility because the Hebrew word for "humility" is a seed lying on the dirt, and, of course, dirt is often brown. Brown could also represent humanism because those looking to help others in their own strength rather than God's tend to look toward the Earth, which is brown, and not up to the heavens. Brown is included in the speckled and spotted in Genesis 30 as the usually less desirable coloring of sheep and goats, which God used to bless Jacob. Another possibility is that brown could represent the downtrodden, who have been trampled to the ground.

Again, with any color, you want to use God's discernment to lead you into the most helpful biblical, cultural, biological, or personal reference for the color in the dream's context.

NUMBERS

Numbers are in the self-referencing symbol category as well. Like colors, they tend to be supportive of other elements in the dream; they could add an attribute of enumeration or some type of timescale.

When the baker and butler had their dreams in Genesis 40, one dream contained three branches and the other three baskets, and both of those signified three days. When Pharaoh had the dreams about the seven cows and seven heads of grain, those represented seven years (Genesis 41).

Though numbers are similar to colors in some ways, understanding numbers can be slightly trickier than understanding colors. Issues of scale, countdown, enumeration, or quantitative and qualitative information will often require greater discernment and revelation.

Where do we get our understanding of numbers? As with colors, we can see the meanings of certain numbers in colloquial usage. How numbers are used in math is also helpful. For example, if you have a dream that contains 3.14 (which is *pi*, the ratio of any circle's circumference to its diameter), it could have something to do with the nature of a circle. Prime numbers, fractions, additions, and subtractions could all potentially mean something that will affect a specific symbol in the dream or the dream as a whole.

As always, we also look to the Bible. There is an incredible richness in the precedent of Scripture, in the verses themselves, in the ancient language, and in the numbered order of God. God does not do things by chance, especially when He orders things. He Himself is in perfect order, and He puts things in perfect order. So numbers have specific issues of order especially as they line up with Scripture. They could tell you things that are unexpected.

If you have a number in a dream, look it up in Scripture, and you will frequently be able to find what it represents. It could be related to the context in which it appears, or it could indicate a verse and chapter number. For instance, if you had the numbers seven and eleven in a dream, it could refer to Luke 7:11, etc. Leaning on the Holy Spirit and practicing your gift of discernment will help you perceive what God is saying. If you dream of a very large number, the meaning could be the *base* of that number. You may not find fifteen million in Scripture, but you will be able to find fifteen. Numbers obviously could also have a literal meaning. A dream about taking the 121 bus could mean that is the route you are meant to take.

Twelve often means authority or rule. There were twelve tribes, twelve apostles, and twenty-four elders: a multiple of twelve. We also see this reflected in measurement conventions. In the English system, there are twelve inches in a ruler.

The number three often represents the Trinity: the Father, Son, and Holy Spirit. When that number appears in a dream, it could be telling us that something is of God. It could also be telling us that something is strong and secure. As Scripture says, a strand of three cords is not easily broken (Ecclesiastes 4:12).

Levitical Law tells us about numbers as well (in the Book of Numbers, for that matter). The Law that God spoke did not have any flaw. It needed to be fulfilled in Jesus Christ, but it was not flawed, so when it says that something is established by two witnesses (Deuteronomy 17:6), we know that the number two can represent a witness. Similarly, when Joseph interpreted Pharaoh's dreams, he said, "Because this happened twice, it is confirmed." So the number two also can represent confirmation or show that something is established and definite. The number two can represent multiplication as well because God created animals male and female. Together the two will multiply. Two also can represent division because when there is more than one opinion, there can be a lack of unity.

All those meanings of the number two are based on biblical precedent alone, and we can see these meanings backed up by the ancient Hebrew pictographs as well. The pictographic character that represents the number two is a tent. In ancient Hebrew culture, what did a tent give shelter to? The family, which multiplies and grows.

The different days of creation will also reveal different things about the meanings of numbers. For instance, we know there is only one God (Mark 12:32) and that God is light (1 John 1:5). On the first day of creation, He said, "Let there be light." This shows that the number one can represent God. In ancient Hebrew, the number one is drawn with an ox head, which means strength, power, or might. These things are descriptive of who God is, His nature; He is the All-Powerful One. So these multiple meanings coincide with one another.

We know that land animals as well as humanity were created on the sixth day, so six is the number of man and of flesh. Scripture tells us that specifically (**Revelation 13:18**), but it also *shows* us why in Genesis.

Creation was completed on the seventh day, the day God rested. By that, we know that seven can represent completion: a full cycle. If you did something seven times in a dream, it might not mean that it will take you seven years to complete or that you actually need to do it seven times; it might represent something that you've done to completion.

As always, the Holy Spirit's guidance is imperative. This is especially true with interpreting numbers. You will need to discern what is relevant in the moment. *Is this dream telling me something about Scripture? Does it mean this verse, which seems to have a positive meaning, or this other verse, which seems to have more of a corrective meaning?* It is very easy to make numbers be what you want them to be and end up with a mind-driven interpretation instead of a Spirit-inspired interpretation. The number should mean what the Holy Spirit says it means through the dream.

When some people see a number in a dream and they don't know what it means, the inclination is to change it in some way so that it will fit, such as adding the individual numbers all together or multiplying them out. But this is only a good idea if the Holy Spirit is clearly leading you to do it. If you dream about the number thirty-four, and every time you think about it, you want to add the three and the four to get seven, seven could be the number God is showing you. However, it isn't good to assume you should add them together like that every time. You shouldn't think, *I don't know what thirty-four means, so let me add the digits together.* That is more of a guess, which will typically lead you in the wrong direction.

There will often be natural breaks or groupings in numbers that can help you see what the number represents or how it should be treated. For instance, if you see 1122, you're seeing two ones and two twos. That is a natural grouping; they are sort of prearranged for you, and the meaning may have to do with the individual meanings of one and two and not 1122 as a whole. Similarly, if you dream about a number that is broken up with commas, you can sometimes treat the numbers before the commas differently than you treat the numbers after the commas. That is a natural grouping, and you aren't interjecting your own groupings or forcing numbers together when you aren't led to do so.

Some people will look at the clock, see a certain time, and know that they are supposed to look up that chapter and verse in a book of the Bible. This may happen with digital clocks in particular because the number is written with a natural break in it. If the time is 2:16, you can see how two could represent a chapter and sixteen could represent a verse. You aren't introducing that or guessing at it; there is a natural break in the number that reflects the way Scripture references are written.

Again, as with colors, numbers will typically *influence* what is in a dream and not necessarily be the most important symbol. They will add context, further specification, or a quantitative or qualitative aspect to something that is already in the dream.

Unless you have keen, practiced discernment, generally stay away from adding, multiplying, or otherwise putting numbers together. Instead, focus on natural groupings, where there could be commas or numbers together.

The inherent understanding that numbers can have meaning is taken out of biblical context in practices such as numerology, which is a New Age system of fortune telling through numbers and numerical sequences. We are not advocating any practice other than what is birthed, given, and interpreted by the Holy Spirit. As always and with everything, rely on His guidance. Take time to listen to Him. Ask Him what things mean, and build your discernment.

NUMBER DREAM EXAMPLE 1:

Martin dreamt that he and several friends were wearing large foam costumes that were shaped like numbers. He was number three but really wanted to be number seven.

Explanation: This dream may be showing something about perceived placement and sequence. Since Martin wants to be seven, it could be referring to the fact that he is ready to be completed or that he wants to finish something instead of just "tri." It could also be showing him that his place is seventh rather than third.

NUMBER DREAM EXAMPLE 2:

Rufus dreamt that he kept seeing the number eight. Then after a little while, he found a house that had the number eight on the door. He went and knocked, and the lady inside said she had been waiting for him for weeks. What had taken him so long?

Explanation: Since eight is the first day of a new week and the day after the completion of creation, it is often seen as the number of new beginnings. This dream is showing the dreamer that he is coming into a place that will be a fresh start.

NUMBER DREAM EXAMPLE 3:

Monica dreamt that she had two babies. After what seemed like just a few days, they had two babies, and soon their two babies each had two babies. This carried on until there seemed to be thousands of babies. But none of them seemed to be growing at all. It was also pretty smelly.

Explanation: This dream is telling the dreamer that she has been very productive in multiplying, but it also gives a warning that more attention needs to be placed on maturing her offspring.

NAMES

Names in a dream can play a significant role in the dream's interpretation. If you have no idea what a certain woman represents in a dream, but her name is Zoe, that could show you the meaning of the element. Zoe means "life."

The Hebrews believed that the essence of a person was in his or her name, or that the name affected the nature of the person. For instance, Hannah[3] means "grace" or "favor." In ancient Hebrew, the name is represented by the symbols ⲙ⳽⳧. These are a picture of a wall, a seed, and someone receiving something. The essential symbolic meaning is to receive seeds from beyond the barrier, and the implication is to receive from God what you can't get on your own. Hannah in the Bible could not conceive; it was beyond her biological ability. But after an encounter in the temple, God sent her provision (seeds) and opened her womb. Hannah was named "grace" by her parents long before her life came to the point of needing and receiving it. This fits with the idea that when you name a child, you are speaking into his or her future and affecting the way that he or she will go about life.

To learn more about names in dreams, we recommend *The Name Book* by Dorothy Astoria,[4] which goes into the etymology of names and the traditional meanings of names, as well as their biblical meanings. You can find links to online etymology sites at www.thedreamsbook.com.

NAME DREAM EXAMPLE 1:

George dreamt that an angel named Ann came to visit his house

---

3 Hebrew chane. Strong's H2584
4 Bethany House, 1997

while he was cooking dinner. She wanted him to know that his children, who were on spring break, would be all right.

Explanation: The root word for *Ann* means "grace." God is giving George grace by taking care of his children and letting him know that they are all right.

NAME DREAM EXAMPLE 2:

Helen dreamt that she was walking down the Cromwell Road in London. It was very quiet. She had the impression that she was to go under the road and get a piece of the foundation to take back with her to the United States.

Explanation: Cromwell means "meandering stream" or "reformer." This dream could be calling the dreamer to become a reformer or to find some other foundational understanding in London. The ascribed meaning of reformer comes from the historical figure Oliver Cromwell.

NAME DREAM EXAMPLE 3:

Steve dreamt that a speaker named Jezebel was coming to his church. She held a large meeting, and many people came, and then they all wanted the pastor to leave the church.

Explanation: Jezebel is a biblical figure who tried to kill all the prophets and turn the people from God. A dream that she is coming to visit is likely a warning about this type of negative spiritual influence.

SHAPES

Shapes often have a meaning based on numbers in their geometry. For example, triangles have three sides and can represent the Trinity. Shapes can often be used metaphorically in reference to everyday objects containing those shapes, as well as in reference to shapes in and related to Scripture.

Shapes and the objects associated with them may also have cultural meaning. In the United States, stop signs are octagons, so an octagon in a dream might mean to stop. Because an octagon has eight sides, it could also mean that there is a new beginning.

Shapes can have meaning based on their physical properties as well. For instance, a circle is the simple form of a wheel that could roll on and on without end, so it could represent unity because it has only one "side." Or it could represent a cyclical event: When you travel in a circle, you keep passing through the same points.

SHAPE DREAM EXAMPLE 1:

Susan had a dream where she was surrounded by overlapping circles everywhere she went. When she made good choices, the circles spun faster, and when she thought bad thoughts, the circles slowed down and started to shrink.

Explanation: Ezekiel 1 talks about "wheels within wheels," which represented the spirits of the creatures next to them. In this dream, Susan was likely seeing the effects of her thoughts and actions on her spirit.

SHAPE DREAM EXAMPLE 2:

Julio had a strange dream one night about leaving a trail of small colored triangles behind him everywhere he went. He knew the triangles were good, but he had no idea what was causing them. When he tried to leave a trail of them on purpose, they stopped following him, but when he would walk without thought of them, they would begin to follow him again.

Explanation: The triangles represent the Trinity: the Father, the Son, and the Holy Spirit. When led by the Spirit, Julio's steps and path are marked by the full nature of God, but it is not his doing, which is why he can't do it on purpose.

SPIRITUAL BEINGS

As we discussed in Chapter Three, the ancient Hebrew understanding of dreams is that when we dream, we are brought close to the boundary of the spiritual realm and glimpse what is happening on the other side. This is backed up by the fact that many dreams recorded in Scripture were encounters with angels. They would give the dreamer direction or a message from God.

Not all spiritual beings you see in dreams will seem like spiritual beings at the time. They could come to you metaphorically or appear as beings you would encounter in the natural. You may find that many *people* in your dreams are actually angels. The word *angel* literally means "messenger," so you could dream about people who come and give you literal messages, directions, or other deliveries that are more metaphorical and will need to be interpreted.

In Acts 16:9, Paul encounters a man from Macedonia in a vision who invited him to come and speak there. Many believe this was actually an angel, who came to Paul in the form of a man.[5]

Just as you could dream about angelic spirits, you could also dream about dark spirits. Scripture says that a third of Heaven fell,[6] and therefore, one out of three spiritual beings is demonic, or fallen. You may come across these in your dreams, typically in nightmares or otherwise dark or negative dreams. They could appear as people, but more likely, they will appear as frightening or aggressive creatures. Some filmmakers say that they have seen the monsters portrayed in their films first in their dreams. Stephen King, the popular horror and science fiction writer, has said that he has entire books based on dreams.[7]

You may also see God in various forms in your dreams — not necessarily face to face, but in clouds and fire and different ways. He may give you a dream in which you don't immediately recognize that He is the One speaking to you. One reason for this is that when we realize God is speaking to us, we often get so excited that we wake ourselves up and aren't able to finish the dream. If you had a dream in which a man showed you the way you should go, that man could have been Jesus, but in the dream

---

5 *For example, John Wesley in his Explanatory Notes*

6 *Revelation 12:4*

7 *Interview* with Stan Nicholls, *SFX Magazine*

you didn't recognize Him in the same way the two disciples didn't recognize Him on the road to Emmaus. In Luke 24:13–35, He was giving them wisdom and teaching them, but they didn't recognize Him until He allowed them to do so. If this is the type of dream you're having, obviously, you really need to pay attention.

There is another type of spiritual being that can appear in your dreams, and this type tends to raise the most questions. You could dream about dead people: grandparents, friends, or people you have never met before, but you are aware that they have died.

Why would you dream about these people? And would it be the real person coming to you, or would it be a metaphor for something else? It could be metaphorical (possibly a root type, based on what the person was or did in natural life); however, it is very possible that the actual person is coming to you as well. This has biblical precedent. In Matthew 17, Jesus met with Moses and Elijah on the Mount of Transfiguration. Elijah never died (2 Kings 2:11), but we know Moses is dead (Joshua 1:2), and Jesus, fully man and fully God, met with them in the natural. Peter, James, and John also saw them. Clearly, Jesus was not participating in necromancy, which is seeking to talk to the dead through demonic or soulish means; it was a God-arranged interaction. Jesus told His disciples to do all He did and more, so if He could do it in the natural, it could certainly happen to us in a dream.

Hebrews 11–12 speaks of the great cloud of witnesses: Christians who have died and are now observing humanity. If your grandparents are a part of the great cloud of witnesses, perhaps God has sent them to *witness* to you concerning issues of wisdom. If a well-known Christian who has died comes to you in a dream, perhaps he or she has been sent to teach you about holiness or some other aspect of God. These experiences should not inspire fear.

I (Zach) was scheduled to teach a class on dreams in London, and before the class began on the first night, a woman came up to me. Fairly concerned, she told me a dream in which she and her husband had gone to a meeting where a famous prophetic person who had passed away was speaking. This person gave her a prophetic word in the dream, and her husband, who remembered the same dream in the morning, had been prayed for and healed of a tendon tear in his shoulder. Her worry was that as this prophetic person had passed away, the dream might not be as positive as it seemed. But God can use such a person to speak to you.

Christian theology makes it clear that when those who know Jesus die physically, their spirits go to be with the Lord. We are with God, and we are alive. Hebrews 12 doesn't specify how the great cloud of witnesses operates, so Scripture leaves the possibility that those people may be used by the Lord in dreams.

On the other hand, you could dream about a dead person who has not been sent to you from God. This is likely a familiar spirit (a demonic spirit that has some type of connection to a person, family, or location) that has come to lead you astray. As always, it is important to be discerning and lean on the Holy Spirit's leading.

You can also dream about living people and have real, actual interactions with them in the spiritual realm. Sometimes, you will even "share" the same dream and be able to remember it. I (Zach) once had a dream in which a friend and I met at a café. The next day, we talked about how we had met at the café in our sleep; we both had had the same dream.

One of the more impacting dreams I (Jim) have had included a friend of mine who was dealing with depression. In the dream, I saw a crack in a wall, and I pulled the crack open. My friend was on the other side, and she was covered in some sort of gray material. I took a hose and hosed her down, and she became brightly colored. The next day I spoke with her in person, and she was clearly doing much better emotionally, and I knew that something substantial had happened in that dream. One historical example of this is Padre Pio, a Franciscan Capuchin priest, who was known to tell people things in their dreams and then later talk to them about it in real life, without them ever mentioning the dream.[8]

What God can do in a dream is not limited, but in this book, we are mainly covering the basic core of what you could see in a dream. Should you have difficulty figuring out what something is or represents in your dream, it could be that you need to expand your horizons and start looking to see if it is something you are not expecting. God, people, angelic beings of all sorts, demons, principalities, members of the great cloud of witnesses — all these can be in your dreams.

SPIRITUAL BEINGS DREAM EXAMPLE 1:

John has a dream where his deceased grandfather shows up and

---

8 *Gaudiose, Prophet of the People: A Biography of Padre Pio*

gives him a message.

Explanation: Because John has descended from his grandfather, this dream could represent his bloodline and blessings that are waiting for him because of the good done by his ancestors, or curses looking to alight from un-repented sin in the past (Exodus 20:5–6). His grandfather could also represent God coming to John in a patriarchal form, or he could be part of the great cloud of witnesses with a message from God.

SPIRITUAL BEINGS DREAM EXAMPLE 2:

Mary has a dream where a missionary currently in China appears to her.

Explanation: This dream could represent a call to pray for the missionary or a call to follow in his footsteps. It could be his guardian angel (Acts 12:15) coming in his form with a burden to intercede for him. God could also be showing Mary the actual man and telling her something about him and his situation.

SPIRITUAL BEINGS DREAM EXAMPLE 3:

Leyla has a dream where one of her children is building a house out of Legos.

Explanation: This could represent a project that Leyla has creatively given birth to and nurtured. The child could represent something born of the flesh that reflects the fleshly nature and not God's nature, or the child could represent the God-given destiny of her child in real life. Leyla could be seeing the child's guardian angel as well.

The area of people and beings in dreams often requires careful discernment and revelation because of the wide range of both good and bad possibilities.

THE UNLOCKING METAPHOR

Some dreams will have a metaphorical key. This is a certain symbol or piece of the dream that helps you to see what the dream means as a whole. As you interpret your own dreams, you will often have a sense of what they mean. You will still have to wade through them, of course, but you know your situation and what you're going through, so you naturally have insight into how the dreams could apply. But when you're interpreting someone else's dream, you aren't as familiar with his or her situation. The key metaphor often will give you a connection with that person. It's an emotional link to the dream that helps you understand the dream.

For example, suppose you are told a dream in which the dreamer is doing a bunch of different activities. He is frustrated in his job; he is working hard, but it doesn't seem to be achieving anything. Later he is at home and trying to make things better, but that isn't working either. Then, in the midst of all the different activities, he goes into the backyard and realizes his puppy is out wandering around.

Even though the puppy isn't there very long, that element helps you realize that the dream is about wandering and looking for purpose and not knowing where you're supposed to be. The

puppy is a mini-echo of the bigger dream and lets you emotionally tap into the dream. A little lost puppy gives you an emotional
feel; as you empathize with it, you realize, *This is what the dream
is about. This is how the dreamer feels — like a little lost puppy.* So
the key metaphor in a dream will often give you an emotional connection to the rest of the dream.

At other times, the key metaphor is less of an emotional
connection and more like the key to a map; when you know what
this specific symbol represents, that understanding will help you
decipher the rest of the dream. The key metaphor isn't necessarily
the most important symbol or metaphor of the dream, just as a
key to a map isn't the most important thing on the map — it is just
extremely important in helping you *understand* the map.

You could dream that you're drowning in a swimming
pool, but at the bottom of the pool, you find a shiny penny. When
you go to interpret this dream, obviously, you'll be able to see that
drowning plays an important role. But at the beginning, it could
be that the only thing you're fully able to interpret is the shiny
penny. So you have to start there. Knowing what the penny represents could release the understanding of everything else.

Because of this, sometimes you won't be able to start
from the most important element (the focus) and work down the
list in order. You may find that you get two or three symbols into
the list before you begin to understand what the first symbols
actually mean.

The final step in interpreting metaphors is going back and
checking them against your dissection of the dream. Sometimes
you'll find that after you've interpreted a couple of the symbols

metaphorically, something you thought was a sub-focus no longer is or that you missed something that will help you interpret the dream as a whole.

When you don't know what something means, it is better to temporarily set that metaphor aside than to pick a default interpretation that doesn't align with the rest of the dream. Once you understand the dream as a whole, you can come back and see how those details fit in. Of course, you should *try* to interpret every element, but if you don't know what something means, interpret the rest of the dream first and come back to that element later. Don't settle on an interpretation unless you have peace and understanding from God. Some dreams also become clearer with time. They can sit with you — and become more tangible as new understanding comes to you.

CHAPTER 9

STEP 5:
DETERMINING NATURE, SCOPE, SOURCE, AND CATEGORY

We are first going to qualify the nature and the scope of dreams in two areas: how literal versus metaphoric they are and whether they address internal or external topics to the dreamer.

LITERAL OR METAPHORIC ELEMENTS

Predominantly, every dream will be ruled either by metaphoric or literal elements. Given that the dreamer is the focus in most dreams, you usually will need to look at the other weighty elements to determine if the nature of the dream is metaphoric or literal overall.

If the activity around the focus is primarily metaphoric, the dream would be metaphoric. If most of the activity is literal, such as resolving problems at work, it would be a mostly literal dream. The interpretation of the latter would be what the dream suggests: You are going to solve problems at work. Keep in mind, however, that when you see the dream coming about in your natural life, the situations that arise may not look *exactly* the way they appeared in the dream.

Most dreams will be a slight mix of metaphoric and literal elements. For instance, you could dream about speaking with your mother, and based on the conversation, you can tell that she is herself in the dream. That part is literal. But the conversation you have with her takes place in the Arctic, which is filled with snow-covered cacti. That is metaphoric.

You may also have dreams that seem to split evenly between literal elements and metaphoric elements, but *usually* one will be more prominent than the other. Use the more prominent classification to determine the nature of the dream.

INTERNAL AND EXTERNAL DREAMS (DETERMINING THE SCOPE OF THE DREAM)[1]

When a dream is internal, it is about you; it speaks to issues that are pertinent to your own life, such as family, friendships, desires, occupations, etc. Typically, this is a dream in which you are the focus, and the interpretation will be specifically about or for you.

An internal dream can include other people as well. Your

---

1 Harris, *Dreams and Experience in Classical Antiquity*

family, friends, neighbors, and even your acquaintances could have active roles in the dream, but you are still at the center of it; the dream is about an issue or situation you are facing. On the other hand, some internal dreams could be expressly for you but have an application for others as well. We call this an internal in-clusive dream.

In an *external* dream, you are typically not the focus, and it is about something or someone other than you. You may be in the dream, but the purpose of the dream doesn't exclusively apply to you. For instance, you could dream about your church. The dream might be about a church issue that has nothing to do with you, or it could include you by association, since you are a member there. So an external dream may or may not include you.

It is important to note the difference between external and internal dreams because this will dramatically affect how the dream is interpreted. Again, most dreams will be about you, but not all of them will be. If you can see that a dream isn't about you, you will be able to interpret it much more accurately.

There may be times when you find yourself wanting to make a dream external when it is really internal. You may be un-comfortable with being the center of attention or prefer to men-tally steer issue-related dreams toward others. So be aware of that. Search for truth and be honest about it. These steps will help you keep on track and remain open to the Holy Spirit's guidance as you interpret.

Finally, as a side note about external dreams, God will sometimes show us what is going on "behind the scenes" with those who have authority over us. He may speak to us about their heart attitudes, decisions they need to make, or areas in which they are struggling so that we can pray for them and potentially take action. It is sometimes easy for us to assume our dreams have a broader application than they actually do, or to rush ahead and tell the official or pastor what God is saying. That may not be necessary or even appropriate. Discernment is vital whenever you feel you have had a dream that has application for leadership, or anyone else. Seek God for wisdom in how you should handle it.

In summary, determining the dream's scope will help you make sure you have the correct interpretation. Clearly address how central you are to the dream. Then, after you interpret it, you can look back and make certain that the symbols and their individual interpretations align correctly. If you know the dream isn't about you, but your interpretation is about you, there is a problem somewhere.

SOURCE

The *source* of the dream will tell you from where, or whom, the dream is coming. If you know where a dream is originating, you will know the purpose behind it, and it will be that much easier to interpret.

The Bible makes it clear that dreams can be from God; however, we are also warned against false prophets who dream dreams they "cause to be dreamed" (Jeremiah 23:32; 29:8). Additionally, we know that the enemy likes to lie, cheat, steal, and counterfeit good things of God. The Bible makes it clear in Ephesians 6:12 that we are in a struggle with spiritual forces of wickedness. The chief of these is identified in Luke 4:2 as the devil, and the Book of Revelation shows that a third of Heaven rebelled with him. So it is important to discern the source of your dream. It could be coming from God, or it could be coming from yourself or the enemy. In some cases, dreams may be coming from more than one of these sources.

DREAMS FROM GOD

Dreams from God are typically characterized by elements that are beyond your understanding or scope of thought. They can coincide with your previous understanding, but when you interpret them, they should give you new revelation and not simply repeat what you already knew.

In many cases, the interpretation of a dream from God will be profound or exciting or seem to have great weight. Your spirit will be able to sense that you just heard from God.

DREAM FROM GOD EXAMPLE:

Giles dreamt that he was in a shop that went on for miles and miles. He went to ask the shopkeeper if they had what he needed, and the shopkeeper said that what he needed Giles already had. He simply needed to learn how to use it.

Explanation: God is sometimes represented by the person carrying the most authority in a certain place. A meeting with a shopkeeper in an overwhelmingly large shop implies something bigger and more special than normal. This is probably a dream about God answering the dreamer's deeper questions.

DREAMS WE CAUSE OURSELVES TO DREAM

The examples in Jeremiah 23:32 and 29:8 of causing yourself to dream is negative; the prophets wanted something to be true, so they dreamt about it. This gave them a sense of credibility with the people:

> "Behold, I am against those who have prophesied false dreams," declares the LORD, "and related them and led My people astray by their falsehoods and reckless boasting; yet I did not send them or command them, nor do they furnish this people the slightest benefit," declares the LORD.
> — Jeremiah 23:32

> For thus says the LORD of hosts, the God of Israel: Do not let your prophets and your diviners who are in your midst deceive you, nor listen to your dreams which you cause to be dreamed.
> — Jeremiah 29:8, NKJV

Unfortunately, Christians in some circles are more likely to do this than non-Christians because we value the appearance of God speaking to us. If you are in a church that listens to dreams, you have a subconscious understanding that if you have a dream, you will be able to share it with other people who will take it seriously.

We often call these *false dreams* — "false" in the sense that they aren't coming from God; they are coming from you, but you may *want* them to be coming from God. Not all of these dreams are negative per se, but they are not necessarily things that God is saying to you.

A common example of this is marriage dreams. Single people will sometimes dream about getting married, or marrying a specific person. If they have a strong desire to be married, it is easy for them to think, *This must be what God is telling me to do.* However, the dream is likely metaphorical in nature, or the dreamer desires marriage to the point that it is affecting what he or she dreams about. Certainly God can use dreams to address issues of marriage, but we recommend great discernment and confirmation.[2]

If you are exceedingly focused on something, you can cause yourself to have a false dream about it. Usually, it will be clear to the people around you when your dreams are coming from your own desires. Your friends and family know you and what you like and want in life; they will usually be able to help you discern when you are trying to rationalize your desires in a dream and when God is giving you direction or understanding. These differences affect the tone and "flavor" of the dream.

All that being said, most of the dreams you have will not

---

2 *If you've had a dream like this, we would caution you not to share your dream with the other person (unless discussing marriage would be appropriate without having had a dream about it). Should you feel the dream was literal, give the situation time, and let life take its natural course. God will be faithful to direct your steps.*

be false dreams. If they are, it is because you have willingly given yourself over to it, as the prophets had in Jeremiah 23:32. Once you have done that, typically your heart will not be concerned if the dream is actually of God or not. So the people who are less likely to do this are the ones who are more concerned with whether or not they have done it.

FALSE DREAM EXAMPLE:

Kyle dreamt that a major prophetic leader passed away the night before he came to town, and Kyle felt that he was supposed to go and speak in his place.

Explanation: This is a dream of dramatic promotion. This dream is revealing a desire in the dreamer to have a big platform without paying the cost that is often involved.

DREAMS FROM NEGATIVE SOURCES

Your dreams can also be caused or influenced by the enemy in an attempt to stop you from walking in God's calling for your life. Dreams from negative sources can include fear dreams and dreams that inspire condemnation or confusion within you. The worst types of these dreams are demonically inspired "false" dreams in which the enemy is lying to you. He tells you something that isn't true or actually going to happen so that you will be deceived.

Another type of dream that deals with a negative source is a flushing dream,[3] which happens after you come in contact with

---

3 Goll, *Dream Language: The Prophetic Power of Dreams, Revelations, and the*

darkness or evil spirits. You could visit a house or city where there is a spirit of greed, for example, and when you go to sleep that night, you could have a dream about being greedy. The dream occurs because your spirit is rejecting what you were exposed to.

NEGATIVE SOURCE EXAMPLE DREAM:

Tommy dreamt that he was watching his girlfriend kissing and dancing with a good friend of his. They seemed to be really happy together, but he was certain that they had never met in real life. The entire dream seemed to be viewed from an old television with bad reception and was sort of yellow and green rather than black and white.

Explanation: God brings clarity and light to issues. More often than not, when colors seem "off" or muted or blurry, the dream is not from God. This is a dream that is attacking a relationship, sowing seeds of doubt and distrust.[4]

MIXED DREAMS

Normally, mixed dreams have several things going on in them. They could contain elements from the enemy as well as elements from God, and often you will be involved in a battle or a fight; you may need to choose what you believe, what you will fight for, or even if you will fight. Mixed dreams can feel like two different dreams from two different sources mixed in the same venue or

---

Spirit of Wisdom
4 *According to Jeremiah 29:11, God has good plans for us that will give us hope, not despair.*

"theater," so to speak. They could have an overall positive message, but certain pieces or scenes could be very negative. For instance, you could dream about slimy frogs that want to go home with you, and in the same dream, there could also be white spots of light that want you to stand in them and be cleansed. Mixed dreams will often present you with a choice.

In conclusion, the source of the dream will help tell you the purpose of the dream, and the purpose will help you determine the category, which we will be talking about in the next section. If the dream has a human source, it has a human purpose. If it has a demonic source, it has a negative purpose. But with dreams that are of God, you can know that their overall purpose is to lead you closer to Him, guide you in your destiny, cause good change in your life, or correct you in a way that will help you move past the things that are holding you back.

Knowing the source of a dream can also help you authenticate or double-check your interpretation. If the dream is from the enemy, it isn't edifying in nature; if it is from God, it isn't meant to cause you fear or condemnation.

DREAM CATEGORIES[5]

The reason we categorize dreams is that it helps us better understand them. It can help give us perspective on dreams, even though only some dreams fit perfectly into one category.

We have organized dreams into five main classifications

---

5 Gnuse, *Dreams and Dream Reports in the Writings of Josephus: A Traditio-Historical Analysis*

that each contain several categories. These are the most common and useful classifications that we have come across. Each of these contains different aspects or kinds of dreams that can come from positive (godly), negative, or human sources.

CLASSIFICATION: SOUL DREAMS

> **Desire dreams**
>
> **Fantasy dreams**
>
> **Flushing dreams**
>
> **Chemical/flesh dreams**
>
> **Rationalization dreams**

CLASSIFICATION: SOUL DREAMS

Soul dreams are primarily self-induced and stem from your wants or unrestrained wishes. If you are thinking about something all the time, you could start dreaming about it.

Soul dreams can also be physiological in nature. As part of the brain's filing system, these dreams help us put things in order, make sense of them, and more easily recall them later. When they are physiological, they are a natural part of processing, so dreamers won't always remember them.

It is possible for dreams in the *soul dreams classification* to originate with the enemy, but generally speaking, you have to be open to a fairly high level of deception for that to happen. The other possibility is that you are in a position of authority where there will be a lot of warfare concerning your decision-making and thought processes. For instance, if you are the President of the United States, you could have a dream in which the enemy tells you, "No, this is all right. You should do this." You yourself haven't necessarily been given to deception, but so many people are trying to influence you, and *they* are promoting deception.

CATEGORY: DESIRE DREAMS

As we mentioned previously, you can be so focused on something that you cause yourself to dream about it. These dreams aren't necessarily "bad," but they tend to leave out God's voice. You are "creating" the dream as a means of processing your wants. For example, if you are thinking about buying an iPad, you could dream about buying an iPad. Your dream isn't necessarily saying you *should* buy one; it is simply reflecting your thought life.

CATEGORY: FANTASY DREAMS

Within the soul dreams classification, you will also find different types of *fantasy dreams*, from those of a sexual nature to those dealing with general desires. They are inspired by the unredeemed part of the soul.

FANTASY DREAM EXAMPLE:

Elizabeth dreamt that she was in a hotel bar, and her husband walked over and told her that she should pursue the man next to her because they were a good match and he would like to see her happy.

Explanation: This genre of dream is not as uncommon as you might think. Among close friends, I (Zach) have heard this theme many times. This is the type of dream that begins to make us feel like it might be all right to move in the wrong direction. Over time, if the idea is not rejected, it could ruin relationships, reputations, and more.

CATEGORY: FLUSHING DREAMS

Flushing dreams fall into the soul dreams classification as well. The analogy of a flushing dream is using the bathroom: You are going through a cleansing process. These dreams often contain both positive and negative elements. Things that aren't of God are being revealed, but there is a God-given process in which they are being taken out of your system. You could experience something demonic in a flushing dream, but God's power is on you to get rid of it.

With flushing dreams, God's cleansing process is similar to pouring water into a dirty cup. When you do that, the dirt floats to the surface. You could have a dream that exposes the stuff you would rather keep hidden. This dream is happening because the Holy Spirit is flushing your system. You aren't seeing these negative things because they are a part of you; you are taking notice of them as they are being flushed away.

Flushing dreams often occur after you have been in an environment where there are lots of people who may be dealing with various levels of darkness and negative spirits. Having this type of dream does not mean that you are doing anything wrong. In fact, it means that you are quickly filtering away negative or unhelpful mindsets. Flushing dreams are different than correction dreams in that God isn't trying to correct something within you; He is showing you what He is removing. A lot of flushing dreams are sexual in nature, and they can be somewhat alarming. But again, these dreams aren't addressing something that is a part of you. You simply came in contact with it, and now it is being flushed out of your system. After the dream, it won't be in you anymore. It is good to recognize where the flushing dream originated and perhaps take heed not to be contaminated with it again, but don't harbor guilt by thinking that what was flushed away remains in you after the dream. As the analogy of a flushing dream is using the bathroom, you don't want to dwell on or examine what you're getting rid of. You just need to know it is happening and then flush it down the drain.

Sometimes, flushing dreams can lead to prayer. After you have spent time with a person who has certain issues or struggles, you could pick up on those issues and have a strong flushing dream to wash them off of you. Now you are more aware of the issues that person is dealing with so you can pray for him or her.

FLUSHING DREAM EXAMPLE:

Joan dreamt that she found a business card in her pocket with the name of a guy who had been hitting on her. There was an appointment to meet up written on the card. It was clear that he had sexual intentions. She threw the card away and wondered how it had gotten there.

Explanation: An encounter from the day before was affecting Joan until God allowed a flushing dream to wash the experience from her spirit. Dreams are not always fully remembered, and if she hadn't remembered throwing the card away in the dream but felt like it was gone, then any issues had not taken hold.

CATEGORY: CHEMICAL DREAMS

Chemical dreams are the result of substances you have taken into your system. Certain chemicals may cause you to be more open to dark or negative influences and therefore to have darker or more negative dreams. Illicit drugs damage your mind, body, and soul, thus affecting your dreams. You could have similar dreams while taking pain medication after a surgery, but they will likely not have the same undercurrents of darkness or rebellion. Consuming large quantities of alcohol or stimulants will also affect your dreams.

CHEMICAL DREAM EXAMPLE:

Brian had a series of dark and incoherent dreams that had scary scenes in them, but the dreams seemed to lack cohesive plots.

Explanation: The dreamer had been taking drugs that

opened him up to dark influences.

CATEGORY: FLESH DREAMS

Like chemical dreams, *flesh dreams* can also originate directly from your body. You may not be able to interpret them; they may simply be telling you that something is going on. If you stepped on a nail and your body hurts, you could dream about that. If you struggle with chemical imbalances, that could affect your dreams as well.

FLESH DREAM EXAMPLE:

Rob had a long series of dreams one night in which he was limping slowly in every scene. He lay in bed the next morning and wondered what the dreams meant. He was completely baffled, even though he had a lot of experience in interpreting dreams. He gave up trying to interpret the dreams that morning, and as he got out of bed, his leg started to hurt from a blow it had received during a basketball game the night before. Rob suspected that the reason he was limping all night in his dreams was because his leg was actually hurt.

Explanation: This pain in Rob's body was influencing his dreams.

CATEGORY: RATIONALIZATION DREAMS

Rationalization dreams will highlight your faults or shortcomings, but they will do it in a way that implies you have a right to them. The dreams seem to suggest, "God is fine with your behavior. You don't need to deal with this." Essentially, these are false dreams that are trying to get you to overlook an issue. For instance, if you are dealing with difficult people at the office, you could have a dream that suggests you don't need to be nice to them or that they deserve your disdain. The purpose of rationalization dreams is to make you feel that God agrees with your negative attitude or actions and that it is all right for you to continue in them.

Rationalization dreams interfere with what would help you become more like God. They give you an excuse and introduce deception into your life. We consider rationalization dreams to be self-inspired dreams, and personally, we think they are prevalent among Christians.

Perhaps you have been doing a negative activity so perpetually that it is sinking into your dreams, and you're rationalizing your behavior in your sleep. Rationalization dreams leave you feeling that you have license to behave in certain ways.

RATIONALIZATION DREAM EXAMPLE:

Amanda dreamt that she was receiving a reward for misleading people about one of her friends. The people offering the reward told her it was all right to lie about her friend because it was in everybody's best interest.

Explanation: The dreamer was rationalizing her bad behavior by pretending that it would have a positive result.

CLASSIFICATION: INTERFERENCE

> Warfare
>
> Attack
>
> Fear
>
> Dark
>
> Deliverance
>
> False

CLASSIFICATION: INTERFERENCE

Interference dreams are dreams that try to keep you from walking in your destiny or knowing the truth. They tend to come from negative spiritual sources, but this is not always the case.

CATEGORY: WARFARE DREAMS

In *warfare dreams*, you participate in or observe spiritual warfare: a battle between dark and light. These dreams usually involve a struggle or some kind of frightening confrontation. There are times when the Lord takes you into warfare dreams to show you where an attack is coming from, to reveal strongholds in your life, or to help you overcome the enemy. You may experience some interference dreams in which you're actually having victory; in that case, the dream is showing you that you are overcoming the interference.

Some of the most impacting dreams I (Jim) have ever had were warfare dreams. When I was a little boy, I dealt with a lot of fear. I would dream about being chased all the time. But one night I had a dream in which I decided I wasn't going to run anymore, even if it meant the evil thing chasing me was going to succeed in catching me. Slowly, starting with that dream, I began to see a chain reaction. I would dream about walking through my house with a six-shooter strapped to my hip. I knew that if something jumped out at me, I was going to have to shoot it. As I determined to become more aggressive with the enemy, I started to dream about walking through my house with the gun in my hand instead of the holster. I was actively looking for the enemy, thinking, *If something is here, I'm going to find it and shoot it.* Then I had a dream about walking through my house with an assault rifle. I stopped wondering whether or not something was there, and I started *wanting* something to be there so I could kill it. That progressed to the point where I would dream about sitting on top of my house with the assault rifle and seeing the entire boundary of my property. I wanted something to appear because I was going to get it when it did. This sequence of dreams showed me how I was overcoming the interference.

WARFARE DREAM EXAMPLE:

Mario dreamt that he was supposed to meet his best friend at the airport and then go to a coffee shop to talk about their future plans. His friend was in the midst of a divorce, so they had a lot to talk about and the friend was in need of Mario's support. Sadly, all of the roads to the airport were closed, and when he tried just to go to the coffee shop in hopes of catching up with his friend there, he discovered that the building had burnt down. In the end, Mario decided to call his friend and they simply talked over the phone.

Explanation: This is a dream that has many obstacles, plans that break down, and difficulties that arise. In this dream, Mario has pressed through and found a way. In many cases, this does not happen, and the dream leaves the dreamer discouraged about what is meant to happen.

CATEGORY: ATTACK DREAMS

Attack dreams can be similar to warfare dreams, but sometimes you aren't actively participating — you're just under attack. At times, they could be quite short. You will be having a dream, and suddenly there will be a snake or scorpion or some other thing coming at you.

Attack dreams reveal something that is trying to take out an aspect of your life. It may be happening in the dream itself: You are being attacked by demons, frightening creatures, evil people, etc. Or it could be something subtle that interferes with your faith.

ATTACK DREAM EXAMPLE:

Jenny dreamt that she was being attacked by monks while on her way to pray at the altar.

Explanation: The dream was trying to establish within her a negative attitude and rejection toward her calling, which has a mystical element to it.

CATEGORY: FEAR DREAMS

Interference dreams can also be *fear dreams.* Children in particular will dream about monsters, evil people trying to get them, being separated from their parents, etc. Unchecked, fear dreams will teach them to run in fear from things that are scary and compel them to stay away from anything that is uncertain. If they dream about a monster in the basement, they may have trouble going into the basement or into other "scary" situations. This could last until they choose to confront that fear.

FEAR DREAM EXAMPLE:

I (Jim) dreamt frequently as a child that I was being chased by dinosaurs. I would run and run and feel like I was never getting away. Then one night during the same reoccurring dream, I decided to stand and not run even if it meant I would be killed. The dream ended when I did that, and it stopped being a reoccurring dream afterward.

Explanation: The enemy was attacking me with fear while I was sleeping — and while I was awake as well, for that matter. This was manifesting in the form of a scary dinosaur that chased me. When I stopped running, I stopped giving room for the fear to affect me, and I was no longer susceptible to that type of fear dream.

As an adult, these dreams try to reinforce your fears and insecurities. You could dream about something happening to your children, ruining a project at work, facing failure or rejection, etc. The point of fear dreams is, simply, to make you afraid in any way possible. They will interfere with you and your relationship with God, as well as your relationships with the people you dreamt about. Demonic forces are empowered by the fear they get from people.

CATEGORY: DARK DREAMS

Like other types of interference dreams, *dark dreams* are usually tainted by negative spirits. They may not feel like a fear or attack dream, but they have negative overtones that can cause you to feel depressed, fearful, anxious, etc.

If you hear the creators behind horror films talk about the inspiration for their work, some of them will say they first saw the monsters portrayed in their films in dreams. Mary Shelley, for example, said that her inspiration for her novel *Frankenstein* came in a waking dream.[6] Christians can experience this category of dreams when they are going through dark times. If you are dealing with such dreams, focus on seeking God before bedtime and avoid dark television and books. Those steps will help.

---

6 Bloom, *Mary Wollstonecraft Shelley*

DARK DREAM EXAMPLE:

Samantha moved with her family to a new apartment complex. During the two years she lived there, she had a reoccurring dream every few weeks about broomsticks, bubbling cauldrons, and creepy vampire bats that bit people and got them to play with the broomsticks and cauldrons. After her family bought a house and moved away, the dreams stopped. Samantha never felt she was being attacked in the dreams, but she always felt "creeped out" after having them. Years later, her mother told her that she once had a conversation with the woman living in the apartment directly under theirs. The woman was a practicing witch and often had others over to participate in her rites.

Explanation: This is a dark dream in which the dreamer is picking up on the dark spiritual atmosphere in the apartment complex during acts of witchcraft. Samantha is not being attacked, but she perceives in her spirit the nature of the activity that is taking place nearby.

CATEGORY: DELIVERANCE DREAMS

Deliverance dreams are dreams that deal with strongholds that we have been struggling with or, in rare cases, actual demonic activity in our lives. Deliverance dreams will tend to have a strong impact. We have seen many people go through these and then stop struggling with various addictions and overcome negative and repetitive behavior. One good friend was constantly dating women who were not the type with whom he could have healthy relationships.

On the surface, things would appear all right, but these relationships were damaging to him. After having a deliverance dream, this pattern changed.

DELIVERANCE DREAM EXAMPLE:

Justin dreamt that he was standing by a large body of water. He wasn't sure if it was a lake, sea, or an ocean. He reached down to touch the water, and this girl he had dated years and years ago came walking across the water. She told him what she had done and why he would never be able to find a healthy relationship. Her mother was right behind her giving her direction. He said he wasn't interested and had moved on. After saying this, he felt a huge weight lift off his shoulders. Then this same girl's grandmother who had just passed away came to him across the water and said he couldn't be free; he was bound to this situation. He said, "In the name of Jesus, I am free, and you have no hold." Suddenly, all three of them flashed away, and he woke up feeling better than he had in several years.

Explanation: This was a deliverance dream in which the soul tie that was created was broken. The soul tie in this case was quite strong, and the breaking had to be reinforced.

CATEGORY: FALSE DREAMS

As an interference dream, a false dream is a counterfeit dream from a negative source that tells you a lie or something that is not of God. Negative sources can be other people, groups, or the demonic realm.

FALSE DREAM EXAMPLE:

A friend of mine once shared three related dreams from one night. In the first dream, he was waiting for the finances to start a business. It looked like all the money was going to be used up before their turn, but when it got to be their turn, there was plenty of money, and they received a huge amount.

In the second dream, which was in black and white, an associate was about to take all the supplies from the office. The dreamer quickly took his own fair share before all the supplies were gone.

In the third dream, the dreamer was a military officer who was about to depart on an important mission. Before he could depart with his team in a plane, he had to wait in line for other planes to take off. But eventually, he did take off in a huge plane.

Explanation: The first and last dreams say the same thing: If he waits patiently, he will get to do what he wants and is called to do, even though it seems like it might not happen. The middle dream says the opposite: He has to take what he needs right now, or he will never get the chance to do anything important. The middle dream seems to be a false dream from the enemy. It lies to the dreamer, telling him he has to take matters into his own hands in contrast to what God is saying. I (Jim) don't think Satan intercepted God's dreams and put a lie in the middle, but I believe that God knew the enemy was sending a false dream and sent a true dream before and after to show my friend His real will in contrast to the lie.

False dreams are dreams that attack the core of who you are and what you are meant to be. They consist of small bits of fact along with much supposition. These sorts of dreams leave us feeling weak and vulnerable if we are not aware of what is happening. Generally, they occur before big events such as important tests, proposals, and times of trials.

CLASSIFICATION: CALLING

Calling dreams beckon to you. They leave you feeling a call to

CLASSIFICATION: CALLING

| Intercession |
| Invention |
| Purpose |
| Correction |
| Action |
| Healing |
| Direction |

something. They inspire change toward your destiny and bring you closer to the will of God. Often, they release hope that circumstances can change and leave you feeling pulled toward an objective.

Calling dreams typically come years, if not decades, before we begin to walk in the calling in its fullness. They can inspire us to study and learn about what we are called to do.

CATEGORY: INTERCESSION DREAMS

Intercession dreams show you what to pray for and often how to pray for it. In a warning dream (which we will talk about later in the chapter), you would typically be told to change or prepare for the consequences, while intercession dreams usually tell you to pray for others and show you the consequences to their lives. We know a mother who had a dream about her child being involved in a car crash. She saw three different outcomes in the dream, and she knew she needed to pray that the crash would happen in a certain way in order to save people's lives. In the dream, she was actually pushing the car three inches to avoid a devastating impact. The forensics team later told her in real life that if the crash had been different by three inches, everyone would have died. Actual intercession often occurs in dreams like these, as was the case in this dream.

CATEGORY: INVENTION DREAMS

Another type of calling dream is the *invention dream*. In Chapter Two, we gave you a short list of dreams that led to breakthrough discoveries in science or other areas. Many of the inventions and revelations of our time have come through dreams. With most invention dreams, the dreamer has a question for which he or she is seeking an answer. For example, Jack Nicklaus wanted to improve his golf swing, and he had a dream that showed him how to do that. He was seeking a specific answer to a specific question.[7]

There is usually a foundation for invention dreams — a longing within the dreamer to discover a particular answer. Most of us don't go to bed one night, have an invention dream, and wake up understanding how to use water in a combustion engine or how to create a more soluble plastic. Usually, you will have an invention dream because you have a God-given desire for something, and you are searching it out.

We sometimes come across people who are praying for invention dreams, and they seem to expect them to contain every detail in a clear and precise way — the complete blueprints. More often than not, however, invention dreams aren't like that. They can be literal, but they also can be very metaphoric. Elias Howe, who invented the sewing machine, dreamt that he was being attacked by people with spears, and the way the spears came in and out inspired his machine. He didn't go to bed and have a dream that gave him specific details of the mechanics; the dream still required a level of revelation and problem solving.[8]

CATEGORY: PURPOSE DREAMS

Purpose dreams are given by God to reveal part of His purpose for the dreamer's life. They can contain a specific calling toward

---

7   *Jack Nicklaus, as told to a San Francisco Chronicle reporter; June 27, 1964*
8   *Kaempffert, A Popular History of American Invention.*

a vocation or can act as a starting point for your moving into the fullness of who you were created to be. They usually convey a great sense of purpose, destiny, and calling. They often impart hope that the revealed purpose can, and should, be accomplished, and after a purpose dream, you will likely feel inspired even before you know the interpretation.

PURPOSE DREAM EXAMPLE:

Rick dreamt that there was a great field in front of him. It was full of people, but all of the people were stuck in mud puddles. Every time they tried to get out, each person would slip and fall back and get covered in mud. Rick went to the first person and helped him get out. It took awhile and was hard, but eventually he was successful. Each person after that became easier to help, and everyone got out more quickly. Eventually, he was also showing people how to wash off the mud. Some of the people he helped followed him around and learned from him how to help others. Pretty soon, the field was full of people helping each other out of the puddles, and Rick only needed to help with some particularly deep puddles.

Explanation: In this dream, a life purpose is revealed by God. Rick is to help others with the situations they are in, and he is to train those who are willing to do the same.

EXAMPLE OF A BIBLICAL CALLING DREAM:

Samuel was lying down in the temple of the LORD where the ark of God was, that the LORD called Samuel; and he said, "Here I am."

Then he ran to Eli and said, "Here I am, for you called me." But he said, "I did not call, lie down again." So he went and lay down.

The LORD called yet again, "Samuel!" So Samuel arose and went to Eli and said, "Here I am, for you called me." But he answered, "I did not call, my son, lie down again."

Now Samuel did not yet know the LORD, nor had the word of the LORD yet been revealed to him. So the LORD called Samuel again for the third time. And he arose and went to Eli and said, "Here I am, for you called me." Then Eli discerned that the LORD was calling the boy.

And Eli said to Samuel, "Go lie down, and it shall be if He calls you, that you shall say, 'Speak, LORD, for Your servant is listening.'" So Samuel went and lay down in his place.

Then the LORD came and stood and called as at other times, "Samuel! Samuel!" And Samuel said, "Speak, for Your servant is listening."

The LORD said to Samuel, "Behold, I am about to do a thing in Israel at which both ears of everyone who hears it will tingle.

"In that day I will carry out against Eli all that I have spoken concerning his house, from beginning to end. For I have told him that I am about to judge his house forever for the iniquity which he knew, because his sons brought a curse on themselves and he did not rebuke them. Therefore I have sworn to the house of Eli that the iniquity of Eli's house shall not be atoned for by sacrifice or offering forever."

— 1 Samuel 3:3–14

Explanation: In this dream, Samuel was awoken on several occasions — he was literally being called by God. In this case, he had to respond in order to receive the calling.

CATEGORY: CORRECTION DREAMS

Simply put, a correction dream is a dream from God correcting a person's actions, beliefs, or attitudes. These dreams are good to have because when you respond to them, you begin to walk in the correct action, belief, or attitude. The appropriate response usually requires repentance, which includes intentional change.

CORRECTION DREAM EXAMPLE:

Stella had a dream one night where she had joined every committee in her church and was involved in every activity going on. At every opportunity, she was helping everybody do things the "right way." As the dream went on, the results from every activity seemed to be worse and worse, and everybody around her was becoming more and more resentful of her.

Upon waking, Stella concluded this dream was telling her that she had God's revelation about what to do, but if people didn't receive God's insight through her, things wouldn't work out right. She continued to believe this interpretation until one day, she shared it with a friend from a different church, who gently told her that she was wrong about the interpretation. The dream said the opposite — because she thought she knew God's will in every area, she was interfering with people who were trying to do what

God had given them to do.

Explanation: This was a correction dream, but the issue being addressed was so entrenched in the dreamer's belief system that it took the kind voice of a friend to help her correctly interpret the dream.

CATEGORY: ACTION DREAMS

Action dreams give you a call to action or some type of information for change that can help set you on the right path. They involve communication from God, and most are telling you to take a certain action. They can reveal the negative attitude you need to leave behind, the positive attitude you should have, the direction you should proceed in, how you should adjust your thought processes or actions, etc. These are the dreams most of us expect or want. God is giving you direction, pulling negative things out of you, and making you more like Him.

Job 33:15–18 says that God gives us dreams but then "seals" them in our hearts to prevent us from pride and sin. Action dreams may be purposely vague or unclear because God is preparing your heart for the place you will be going, rather than the place you are in currently. If you knew your full destiny, you might try to race forward and get there on your own and miss some of the most important parts of it: maturing in God, realizing His goodness and faithfulness, and growing more and more in love with Him. Your destiny is made up of the *steps* to the end point and not simply the end point itself.

ACTION DREAM EXAMPLE:

David dreamt that he was walking toward a large stone that had "My Calling" written on it, with an arrow showing the direction he was to go. He stopped to wait until he was strong enough to carry the stone. This stone was worn around the edges from all the people who had tried to pick it up before him. A voice said, "You don't have to lift it; you simply have to start walking in the right direction."

Explanation: This is a dream in which the dreamer is directed to act and move toward his calling.

CATEGORY: HEALING DREAMS

Healing dreams are dreams that produce a healing or give insight into how the dreamer or someone else will be healed. Miraculous healing dreams, where physical healing takes place in the dream, are not very common, but they do occur. Healing dreams also relate to emotional healing that can remove very old scars and mend relationships.

HEALING DREAM EXAMPLE:

Steffen (who was deaf) dreamt that he was being prayed for at a church. The assistant pastor prayed for him and nothing happened. He left the building, and a little girl came up to him and said in a sweet voice, "God says you don't need those," referring to his hearing aids that he wore only so people knew he couldn't hear. She then kicked him in the shin, and suddenly he could hear everything. When he woke up, he had been healed. He could hear very loud noises outside his building and knew that he was going to have to find a quieter apartment.

Explanation: The dreamer was healed in this dream from a lifelong condition.

CATEGORY: DIRECTION DREAMS

Direction dreams give you direction. You could have a dream about moving to Alaska not because it is metaphorical in some way, but because God is saying He wants you to move to Alaska. You could dream about buying a certain type of car because that is the car God wants you to have or because it represents some activity that you are supposed to engage in. Metaphorically, direction dreams once interpreted will point in the direction that you are to head. God could also give you a direction dream as part of the confirmation that you are to do something specific. Direction dreams show you what God wants you to do.

DIRECTION DREAM EXAMPLE:

Kevin had a dream where he was at work. When he checked his email, he saw one from the CEO telling him to use the emergency exit door and take all his personal belongings with him, but not anything that was work related. Kevin has this dream three nights in a row, and each one felt more urgent than the one before.

Explanation: God, Kevin's ultimate CEO, is directing him to leave his job quickly, and God is confirming this with multiple dreams and a great sense of urgency. As with all dreams that involve massive changes in life, it is good to pray and seek secondary confirmation.

CLASSIFICATION: REVELATION

Prophecy	Knowledge
Condition	Understaing
Stronghold	Mixed
Encouragement	Lucid
Warning	

CLASSIFICATION: REVELATION

This class of dreams tells you what is going on currently and what will or could happen in the future. If the dream is telling you something about your current circumstances, it will often seem more informational in nature, almost like a news bulletin. It is supplying you with this information so that you will understand the mind of God or His perspective of the situation.

It is impossible to know something of God without it changing you. Depending on what He is doing, a revelation dream may not give you actual "direction," but it is letting you know something that you can act on or pray about, so that when the time comes and the situation appears, you will be able to respond accordingly.

With revelation dreams, you need to be aware of two important things: the weight of the choice presented to you in the dream and the clarity of the dream. If God appears to you in a dream and tells you to do something, and you know without doubt that it really is God and His directions are explicit, then do it and do it well. However, many direction or prophetic dreams lay groundwork for the decision you *will be* making. They help prepare your heart, so that when it comes time for you to make the decision or take the action, you will be able to submit to God and His leading. As many dreams are highly metaphoric and unclear, it would be unwise to make massive life-changing decisions based on them alone.

CATEGORY: PROPHECY DREAMS

As part of the revelation dreams classification, *prophecy dreams* will tell you what is going to come to pass: your future, the future of someone else, the future of your church, or even the future of your town or nation. Prophetic fulfillment is not always a certainty, however; there are often conditional factors relating to much of the prophecy that is received.

PROPHECY DREAM EXAMPLE:

Wendy dreamt that she was moving to a new house in a town that she had never visited. In her dream, the house had three stories and was made of gray granite. Three months later, she moved into this house.

Explanation: This dream was fairly literal, although there may be some secondary metaphoric content. Had this specific dream been only metaphorically interpreted (rather than literally), the interpretation would have likely been wrong.

CATEGORY: CONDITION DREAMS

Condition dreams show you God's perspective of your current state. Many times, condition dreams help you understand why you are in your current situation, and they are revelatory in the sense that you are gaining a better perspective.

For example, you could dream that you're running on a treadmill, and the faster you run, the faster it goes, and you never get anywhere. This dream could be showing you your current condition by highlighting your frustration. It does not do this so that you will think, *God wants me to be frustrated. This treadmill is my destiny.* No, the purpose of the dream is to show you that God sees the way you feel. He knows, and therefore, you can have hope. Once you realize that God sees your problem, you may have enough faith to cry out to Him to change it, which is probably why you had the dream.

Sometimes, these dreams will show you something you didn't realize at all, and at other times, they may give you perspective on your actions or beliefs. For instance, you could dream that you are walking around and putting rocks in people's backpacks.

It would seem that something you are doing is not a positive, life-giving activity.

It is very important not to confuse this type of dream with a direction dream. God isn't saying, "This is the way it is supposed to be." Instead, He is pointing out your current condition so that you can have His perspective on it and potentially take action based on what He has shown you.

CONDITION DREAM EXAMPLE 1:

Hugh dreamt that he was in a revolving door going around and around and around, again and again. Every once in a while, it occurred to him to get out of the door, but he compulsively chose to keep going in circles.

Explanation: This dream doesn't show that he has to stay in a repeating pattern. It shows that he is stuck until he starts making different choices.

CONDITION DREAM EXAMPLE 2:

Peter dreamt that he was surfing on a really nice wave. But his board was missing its fin, so he couldn't control where he was going and ended up falling a lot more than he should have. It was really frustrating.

Explanation: The dreamer is in a good place, but he is lacking some of the tools to take advantage of the situation. God is showing him that he is wandering and in search of direction, which are making him less effective.

CATEGORY: STRONGHOLD DREAMS

Stronghold dreams address various things in your life that you wouldn't be comfortable with or willing to address while you are awake. With this type of dream, the important thing to consider is the potentially positive outcome. The dreams can give you the inspiration you need to deal with issues you would rather ignore.

With stronghold dreams, God isn't necessarily showing you your strongholds. Instead, He may be showing you where your strongholds are manifesting themselves — blocking you from truth or ruling over you.

The primary nuance between correction and stronghold dreams is that correction dreams tell you how to change while stronghold dreams show you what needs to change. In contrast, rationalization dreams encourage you to hang on to things that both stronghold and correction dreams urge you to change.

STRONGHOLD DREAM EXAMPLE:

Michael dreamt that he was in a house with some old friends. They were having a talk with his sister about racism. He was trying to defend her negative attitude toward various other people groups. The friends then turned to him and said that this was something that he needed to deal with as well.

Explanation: This is a dream where the dreamer is finding strength in someone else's view. But it is a view that is clearly wrong. In the dream, Michael is told he is wrong, which addresses the stronghold.

CATEGORY: ENCOURAGEMENT DREAMS

Encouragement dreams can help you realize that God is with you in your situation. They encourage you based on that understanding.

For instance, in an encouragement dream, you could dream about something you are going to do or are already doing, and afterward, you wake up feeling more encouraged in moving forward. Or you could be feeling uncertain about a choice you've made, and the dream shows you that you made the right choice. It gives you confirmation.

ENCOURAGEMENT DREAM EXAMPLE 1:

Judith dreamt that she was planning to move across the ocean to another country. This had been on her waking mind for several days. As the dream continued, she watched herself moving into her new house and saw a rainbow settle right over the house. She woke up knowing that she was doing the right thing.

Explanation: This was an encouragement dream that showed a positive affirmation for an action the dreamer was already considering.

ENCOURAGEMENT DREAM EXAMPLE 2:

Josiah dreamt that he was halfway through a big math test, and he knew he was getting most of the problems wrong. But as he decided that he needed to finish the test even if he failed it, the problems started becoming easier, and he was able to answer them quickly — so quickly, in fact, that he was able to go back to the earlier questions and redo them.

Explanation: God is encouraging Josiah that if he doesn't give up, not only will he finish the test that he is in, but he will pass it with flying colors. This is very encouraging to Josiah, who, until this dream, felt stuck in life and like a failure.

CATEGORY: WARNING DREAMS

Warning dreams give you insight into situations that you will need to avoid or be prepared for. They let you know that if you proceed down a certain path, it could be dangerous or difficult. In other words, they give you a heads-up so that you can make an informed decision. God will also warn you before He lets your own decisions bring judgment upon you; this is an act of grace that should be responded to quickly. A warning dream implies that it is possible to change to avoid the consequences shown in the dream, or that it is possible to be prepared for them.

In September 2001, I (Jim) had friends who had dreams warning them about going to work. These people worked in the financial district of New York City, and on the morning of September 11, they didn't go to work because of what they had dreamt. The dreams weren't showing them how to prevent the terrorist attack, but they warned the dreamers, thus protecting them.

WARNING DREAM EXAMPLE:

Matt dreamt that he was driving to work one morning. While driving, he saw a large pickup truck branded with the name of a company that was recruiting him. It suddenly swerved into him in a violent, aggressive way and made him crash into a tree on the side of the road.

Explanation: This is a warning that coming in close contact with this company will not end well for the dreamer.

CATEGORY: KNOWLEDGE DREAMS

The gift of prophecy is often broken into two primary areas: prophetic words and words of knowledge. The prophetic speaks about things that have not yet happened — future possible events. The word of knowledge, on the other hand, speaks of things that are happening, have happened, and clear, undisputable facts. Knowledge dreams are similar; they sometimes need little interpretation because they present the dreamer with fact. It is possible that some of these dreams will be metaphoric but will reveal fact when interpreted.

KNOWLEDGE DREAM EXAMPLE:

Anita dreamt that she saw her husband walk into his home at 100 Atlantic Drive in a city on the coast. She didn't understand until she talked to him about it. That was one of the homes he had lived in as a young child. After that, he started paying more attention to dreams.

Explanation: Like words of knowledge, knowledge dreams make people pay attention. They contain fact that can be verified and will cause people to listen or be concerned in the future.

CATEGORY: UNDERSTANDING DREAMS

Understanding dreams reveal the ways of God and His nature. This includes the application of wisdom and how God has made all of creation to work.

UNDERSTANDING DREAM EXAMPLE:

Scott dreamt that he was in a space ship and saw a giant heart. As he tried to navigate around it, he realized the heart was getting bigger and bigger. He heard a voice say, "You cannot measure my love."

Explanation: As a result of this dream, the dreamer has a better understanding of the infinite nature of God's love.

In conclusion, if you know the *source* of a dream, you can know its general purpose. If you know the *category* of a dream, you will have a better understanding of what it could mean. Dreams from God (calling and revelation dreams) will bring change to your life in positive ways; dreams from the enemy (interference dreams) will try to discourage you or otherwise keep you from walking in all that God has for you. Dreams that you cause yourself to dream (soul dreams) will sometimes reinforce negative behavior or help you process your day.

Understanding dream sources and categories will help you as you go to interpret the dream.

DREAMS BELONGING TO MULTIPLE CATEGORIES

Dreams can belong to or have scenes that are part of more than one category. You might have difficulty in finding a single category for a dream. Sometimes to fully understand the dream, you will need to identify all the categories involved.

LUCID DREAMS[9]

The word *lucid* means "clear." When you are having a lucid dream, you tend to have enough presence of mind to be aware that you are dreaming. There are two factors of lucidity in dreams: how aware you are in the dream and then if you are making decisions in the dream. These factors can occur on a broad spectrum, from intense to mild.

It is important to know whether or not you are lucid dreaming because if you are semi-aware within the dream, you are capable of having independent thoughts that are not part of the dream. For example, you could dream about working in the garden with your parents, but while you are doing that, you start worrying about something you're worrying about in your natural life. The dream could be from God, but the thoughts you are having might not be. You want to discern that and separate the two so that you won't try to interpret them together.

Second, lucid dreaming allows you to be alert enough to make real decisions in your sleep. You could have a current condition dream in which God shows you that you have bitterness

---

9 Oldis, *The Lucid Dream Manifesto*

toward someone. In the dream, you can repent, and when you wake up, there is no bitterness anymore. Or if you are having a fear dream, you can turn and face your fears. If you are having a warfare dream, you can start fighting with more faith and start winning. These are real decisions.

Lucid dreaming can allow you to respond appropriately during the dream. As you grow in lucid dreaming, you will find that you can make decisions about your life based on what God is showing you and potentially even interpret the dream while you are dreaming it. Any use of your God-given freewill to make godly choices is good, no matter when it happens.

At first, it may seem a little odd to lucid dream. It may be slightly confusing and disorienting as it happens, but it is actually rather natural. You may even realize you are dreaming and accidentally wake yourself up, but as you cultivate God's peace in your life and even in your dreams, that will dissipate. Again, you want to make godly decisions in any area where God has given you awareness and the capability of making decisions.

An aspect of lucid dreaming is that it can allow you to reenter dreams. If you are in the middle of a dream from God and wake up from it, it is a form of lucid dreaming to go back into the dream. The best way to do this is by reviewing the plot and action of the dream as if you were still dreaming it, and addressing what you think different elements mean while you are falling back asleep. Typically, the dream resumes where it left off. This may take some practice, but it should become easier once you have done it a few times.

There are a lot of different opinions from secular psychology and New Age practices about lucid dreaming and controlling what you want to happen within the dream; those we are not advocating or articulating. When we speak of lucid dreaming, we mean cooperating with the Holy Spirit, remembering dreams you have forgotten, going back into dreams you awoke from, and making godly decisions in dreams. You could develop skill at dictating dreams according to your soul, but that is not what we are talking about. Lucid dreaming is a positive experience only if you are cooperating with the Holy Spirit.

FULLY LUCID DREAM EXAMPLE:

Celia had a dream where she was shopping for her family at the supermarket. She was aware that she was dreaming and knew she needed to make good choices for her family. She looked in the basket and saw that she had selected some boxes of cereal that had lots of sugar in them. Recalling that in real life her children had seemed to have less energy during the late mornings, she decided to change what was happening in the dream. She went back to the cereal aisle and put back the cereal she had previously chosen. She then decided to further change the eating patterns of her family by getting organic fruits and vegetables instead of preprocessed food.

Explanation: Celia had a dream where she became fully lucid, aware that she was dreaming, aware of events outside the dream, and able to make intentional choices that changed what was going on in the dream. The choices she made in the dream carried over into her awaking life.

PARTIALLY LUCID DREAM EXAMPLE:

Jorge dreamt that he was playing baseball with his son Michael. He was aware that he was dreaming and that it was not "real life." The dream continued as it did before, but every once in a while, Jorge contemplated the fact that he was dreaming.

Explanation: Jorge is only partially lucid. He is aware that he is dreaming but is not making any choices that affect what is happening in the dream.

CHAPTER 10

STEP 6:
INTERPRETING THE DREAM

In this step of the interpretive process, you begin to tie together the various elements of the dream. You address why the dream was given, its purpose, and the core message of what it is saying. This step has three stages or sections involved: the rough interpretation, the final interpretation, and then the communication of the final interpretation. Often when you communicate an interpretation, you do all these steps at once, but we are breaking them down into three stages so we can be intentional about it and further concentrate on the areas that may need improvement.

THE ROUGH INTERPRETATION

The rough interpretation is an initial draft that helps you get your thoughts together before you craft a final interpretation that can be presented to others.

Throughout the interpretive process, bits and pieces of the internal interpretation have probably been coming together in your head. *What if this means this? What if this part and that part have this meaning when considered together?* At this step of the interpretive process, you actually put together the thoughts you have been considering. This interpretation doesn't have to be smooth or refined yet; it is more of a reference point that helps you move forward. At this phase, focus on two basic things: laying out the different elements in a way that makes sense and being certain that the full meaning of the dream is conveyed.

The rough interpretation is especially helpful if you are interpreting a dream for someone else. For some people, the worry over what they are going to say can interfere with their ability to listen to the Holy Spirit. They could be nervous or feel such pressure that they aren't open to hearing from God in the moment. But if they know they can piece together an "internal sketch" at the beginning and then make it clear later, this helps them have peace and do a better job overall.

With the rough interpretation, you have an understanding of the dream based on the interpretation of the symbols, but you aren't yet ready to share it with other people. For one, it might not be very clear, but also, there may be certain things the dream contains that are not fit for communication. If you are interpreting a dream for someone else and the dream clearly portrays the dreamer as controlling and manipulative, your rough interpretation could be to the point and forthright: "You are controlling and manipulative." But when it comes time to give the person your interpretation, you could say, "This dream shows that you are in a battle to fight how much control you're going to exert and how much manipulation goes on around you." This says the same thing but does so in an edifying way.

Finally, there may be times when you need to compose a rough interpretation that isn't entirely complete. For instance, perhaps the dream contains some elements that are going to require a deeper level of discernment to interpret. Or perhaps you know what three of the elements mean in relation to one another, but you don't know about the remaining two. This is the step where you would begin to feel God's peace and realize, for example, that the dream isn't as bad as you thought, or that you know *most* of what it means, just not the timing or the place. Sometimes these final elements will come together as you do the rough interpretation. You may not know what they mean at the beginning, but God reveals them to you as you move forward. The point with this step is to put in place what you do know about the dream, so that if you review the interpretation later, your understanding will come back to you.

INTERNAL INTERPRETATION EXAMPLE:

Mara was on a dream outreach team at a church conference interpreting dreams for attendees. One woman sat down and told Mara how she dreamt that she was an octopus trying to touch every activity that was going on with her tentacles. Mara said to herself, *Even though the dreamer thinks this is a good dream, it says that she is operating with a Jezebel spirit, trying to control and manipulate everything going on in the dream.* Mara knew what the dream meant, but she also knew she had to use much more sensitive and delicate wording with the dreamer if she wanted her to be able to respond positively to the dream.

THE FINAL INTERPRETATION

The final interpretation differs from the rough interpretation in that at the end of this step, you have an interpretation that is clear, appropriate, and ready to be communicated.

Depending on the dream, the final interpretation could look very different than what you put together in the rough interpretation step. It should communicate the same core message, but you need to be sympathetic. Consider what should and should not be said and how the interpretation will affect the listener.

For instance, God might give you a dream that says your coworkers need to be nicer to you. Before you share that with them, you would first need to make certain your words are edifying and receivable; otherwise, you could end up just heightening the tension. Perhaps your final interpretation could say, "I had a dream that shows we're having conflict, and we need to find some way to be at peace."

With the rough interpretation, you have the freedom to put together your first impression of the dream's meaning. This might be harsh or abrasive depending on the dream. But with the "edited" interpretation, others should be able to read it or hear it and respond positively. The prepared interpretation reflects your understanding of how this dream fits into God's heart.

KEEP YOUR INTERPRETATION FOCUSED

There are a few issues involved with preparing an interpretation for other people. The first is presenting it in a way that is clear. Be sure you have understood the dream's purpose and that the interpretation conveys the dream's core meaning. One way to double-check this is by re-familiarizing yourself with the pertinent dream nature, scope, category, and source and being sure that your interpretation aligns with them. Another way to cross check is to review the dream while reading the interpretation and make sure that nothing is missing or out of context.

If you spend time with other dream interpreters, you will begin to notice that we all have strengths and weaknesses. Some interpreters seem to receive understanding more easily, and some are able to communicate more easily. If you do well with receiving revelation but have a hard time communicating it, you may find yourself consistently bogged down as you try to speak to the dreamer. It could be helpful for you to familiarize yourself with others' interpretations and see what standardized introductions work well for them:

> "God gave you this dream because . . ."
> "You had this dream because . . ."
> "The main point (focus) of this dream is . . ."

Along with this, be sure to use language that will help others understand the dream. For instance, if you are interpreting the dream of a young child, your language needs to be appropriate for that age and use words that he or she will be able to understand easily.

The final interpretation is important even if you are interpreting your own dream and don't intend to share it with anyone. It helps develop a skill that will come in handy when you do share a dream with others or go to interpret someone else's dream.

WEIGH THE IMPACT

When you have the correct interpretation, you should be able to feel it in your spirit. There should be some sort of *release* within you that causes you to realize, "Yes, *this* is what the dream means." When the Holy Spirit confirms the answer in your spirit, it will often feel this way.

In music, a certain sequence of notes can cause an almost physical need for resolution. If the music does not resolve itself, the listeners will feel that they have been left hanging. Similarly, the right interpretation should *resolve* the dream. The release should still be there even if the dream is communicating something that may be difficult to hear. The dreamer will think, *This means I will have to make changes in my life, but at least I know now what God is saying.*

In the interpretive process, you aren't simply asking, "What interpretation sounds meaningful and impacting?" You are more precisely asking, "What interpretation brings release from the Holy Spirit?" That is what you are aiming for. When you are interpreting dreams for other people, you are essentially functioning in a priestly role of helping people have peace with God. You are also helping dreamers come into deeper understanding of God. You will often see a physical response as the interpretation hits them — a relaxation in their shoulders or postures. They may say something like, "Wow. That makes sense." When an interpretation is right on, the dreamer almost can't avoid sensing some sort of peaceful response to it in his or her spirit. That is part of weighing the impact. There may be times when you meet people who are cynical about dream interpretation or, perhaps, just *you* interpreting their dreams. But even then, you could see a reaction as the interpretation impacts them.

Assess the impact the interpretation is having on you. Did it release a sense of peace? Is there a witness in your spirit? Can you tell that you have at least touched on the *core* of what the dream means? This is significant, because as you interpret dreams and sense the Holy Spirit's confirmation, you will learn more about God and how He speaks. The process you took with the Holy Spirit to get there will become more and more natural. Usually, if you don't feel a release, the interpretation probably needs more work or possibly time.

FINAL INTERPRETATION EXAMPLE:

In the previous dream about the octopus, Mara's rough interpretation said that the dreamer was operating in a controlling and manipulative way. But Mara decided to tell the dreamer, "God is telling you in this dream that you think you need to be involved in everything that is going on in your church, that you feel every situation needs your help. He is using this dream to remind you that He is God and needs you to do only what you are responsible for and to trust Him with what everybody else is doing."

Explanation: This interpretation conveys the core message of the dream — to stop controlling and manipulating everything that is going on — in a way that doesn't condemn the dreamer but does call her to respond to the inherent correction of the dream.

INTERPRETATION FEEDBACK

Receiving feedback is an important part of growing in the interpretive process. However, that won't be possible or even necessarily acceptable in certain situations. When you are interpreting your own dreams, you can seek out feedback from other interpreters. However, when you are interpreting dreams that are not your own, the dreamers often won't be prepared to give you the sort of feedback you're looking for. It takes time to be aware of the full impact of an interpretation. There are occasions when it is instantaneous, but more often, it is a process. So in some cases, the best feedback you will receive is seeing the Holy Spirit's response in the other person.

The second best feedback can come from interpreting dreams as a team; you can coach each other about the language and tone of the interpretation and how it could have been better.

After you have sensed the Holy Spirit's release and believe you have the correct interpretation, there are still a few questions you need to answer before you are ready to communicate that interpretation. Consider the situation and the setting and determine whether or not you are ready to proceed. If you are interpreting a child's dream, do you have the parents' permission? If a coworker told you a dream, is the person prepared to respond to the interpretation in a healthy way? How will this interpretation impact the dreamer? Do you have favor to communicate it with him or her?

COMMUNICATING THE DREAM

In this section, we will be going over some practical steps for communicating the interpretation of a dream. In general, it is important to keep your interpretation relatively short and to the point. This gives the other person the opportunity to remember the core meaning or to ask follow-up questions, which suggests that he or she is open to hearing more. If the dreamer doesn't ask questions after your short summary, he or she probably wouldn't have wanted to hear the long version. So be concise and to the point.

HAVE INTEGRITY IN THE COMMUNICATION

Be sure that what you are sharing with the dreamer is the actual interpretation of the dream. It may seem unnecessary to say that, but it is an issue of integrity. If you tell someone, "This is the interpretation of your dream," be careful it doesn't also contain your opinion or advice. One of the surest ways to ruin a dream interpretation is to confuse it with counseling the person. After you have interpreted a dream well and there is release and impact, the other person could be very open to what you have to say, but this isn't the time to take advantage of that. Trust is built as you are faithful to present only what God has told you and not your own opinion.

If you do this, you will grow in favor with that person.

Based on biblical precedent, we know that some dreams will have an additional application — something that is above and beyond the interpretation itself. Again, this is the application that *God* reveals to you; it is still revelation and not your own opinion or advice.

In the case of Pharaoh and Joseph, the basic interpretation of Pharaoh's dreams was that there would be seven years of plenty followed by seven years of want. Only after he had explained the dreams' meaning did Joseph give Pharaoh the application: "This is what you should do about it." Sometimes when you interpret a dream, God will give you a follow-up application. Ideally, the best time to share that is if the dreamer asks you questions or seems to be seeking additional information. Be sure you don't present it as part of the dream itself.

God gave that person the dream for a reason. As the interpreter, it is your job to explain what that reason is. Then, if you have more to say, be sure the person knows that what you are adding isn't part of the actual interpretation; it is additional information. All the things you may know about the person or the situation could be communicated as "extra things" in a follow-up conversation. It is not our place to help God by adding in what we think He left out of a dream. It is better if additional conversation is sparked by the dreamer's interest and not the interpreter's enthusiasm. You can tell if this has happened because the dreamer will ask questions and not appear as if he or she is just waiting for you to stop talking.

If you are communicating with the dreamer via email or

some other written form, be specific about what is part of the interpretation and what is not, and share any additional revelation *after* the interpretation of the dream.

STAY TRUE TO THE WEIGHT OF THE DREAM

There is a subtle difference between interpreting a dream in a language the dreamer understands and interpreting the dream in a language the dreamer wants. Dreamers may be looking to hear certain things. For instance, some people may want to hear that they are important to the future of an organization or in a leader's life. But that may not be what the dream communicates.

If your friend dreams that she is ignoring a starving dog that keeps coming to her door, God could be telling her that she needs to be more considerate. Said with care, that should be the interpretation: "I think/feel that God gave you this dream because He wants you to be more considerate." It is important not to make the dream bigger than it actually is. You don't have to add additional weight to the interpretation by saying, "God gave you this dream to show you how consideration will lead you to your destiny." The dream could have great impact, or it could be just one in a series of dreams that draws her attention to something gently. Keep in mind that by interpreting others' dreams, you are fulfilling your role of bringing truth to someone else on God's behalf. You're not doing this to make others happy with you; you're doing this to be helpful.

If keeping your interpretation clear or on track is an area of difficulty for you, you may want to use certain sentences that can help you stay focused, such as, "God gave you this dream for this reason."

Make sure that your first few sentences clearly state the dream's purpose:

"You had this dream to show you that you need more sleep."

"You had this dream to show you that you need to be more thankful."

"You had this dream to show you that God is really pleased with you."

If you make purposeful statements like these, you'll tend to follow them up with other sentences that better fit the dream.

Stay true to the weight of the dream and clearly communicate the interpretation in its completeness. If you have only bits and pieces of the interpretation, let the dreamer know that, and try not to present the interpretation as more than it is.

BE SENSITIVE TO LANGUAGE

When you are sharing a dream's interpretation, choose language that will best communicate what the dream means to the specific person or people you are addressing. If they are of a different culture, generation, language, or value system, be sure to use words that they can understand. Avoid language that will confuse them.

If you are interpreting a Christian's dream, the quickest way to fail in getting your point across is by adding religious terms. It is better to say something plainly and simply than to load it with religious pretense.

Suppose this dream was given to you for an interpretation:

I dreamt that I was walking and slipped and fell in the mud. My shirt was filthy. I tried to get it clean, but I couldn't. Then a man appeared and helped me with it.

It would be a fairly simple matter to fill this dream with religious overtones: "This dream shows that you are in sin, and you need Jesus to redeem and sanctify your life because you can't purify it on your own." That interpretation isn't entirely wrong, but it isn't as clear and understandable as something more simply stated: "This dream shows that there is stuff in your life that you know isn't good. You want to get it out, but you're going to need Jesus to do it for you."

Often, people use religious terms or spiritual jargon to suggest that they have more understanding than they actually do. If you say, "This dream is about sanctification," it leads others to believe that you understand sanctification. But if you say, "This dream is about making your life right," you are not trying to impress the dreamer with mysterious religious knowledge; you are trying to give him or her clear understanding.

BE AWARE OF THE ENVIRONMENT

Where are you interpreting dreams? Is it in the church or on an outreach? Is this for a Christian or for a Muslim? Is it for a man or for a woman? All these things can affect how the dream should be communicated.

In a way, the dream itself will let you know how you should communicate the interpretation. If God is hidden in a dream, it could be that the dream carries weight and anointing, and He wants the dreamer to search Him out (Proverbs 25:2). But if you are interpreting dreams in an outreach setting, God could be hidden in the dream because the dreamer is at a spiritual level where He needs to be hidden — that is, the person is willing to hear from Him only when his or her mind doesn't know it is Him. In that instance, your role is to give the person enough understanding so that he or she can move forward; the dream is a gentle nudge on the person's heart.

During an outreach a few years ago, I (Jim) met a man who'd been having a recurring dream about standing on a bridge that was leading over a cliff. He wanted to cross, but he didn't know where the bridge was headed. I knew that Jesus was beckoning to him in this dream, but I didn't mention that, because I also sensed that he was struggling with issues of God. So I told him what the dream clearly stated: It was calling him to step into things that were different. Essentially, the dream was a call to change.

If Jesus had been in the dream in a clear way, I would have communicated that. But the dream did not specifically state that the invitation was from God; it was just encouraging the man to take a step forward, and if he did, he would eventually realize God was waiting for him.

Again, when God isn't in a dream clearly, it may be because the person isn't ready to knowingly hear from Him yet. God knows what that person needs to hear, so there is a reason He chose to reveal Himself the way He did. We shouldn't try to put Him into the interpretation in a way that He didn't appear in the dream.

There is a biblical precedent for not immediately revealing Jesus in certain situations. When Jesus spoke to people in the Gospels, He would sometimes create a hunger that brought them back for more. He would allow them to ask questions. For instance, He told the woman at the well, "I have water you don't know about." He didn't say, "I'm Jesus, the Son of God. Here are the four spiritual laws, and by the way, this water represents Me." That might have overwhelmed her and caused her to shut down. Instead, He used plain language and captured her attention by intriguing her (John 4).

In the same way, you should use plain language as you interpret dreams. If the dream about the muddy shirt was told to you in an outreach setting, you could say, "This dream is showing you that you need to clean up your life, but you're going to need help to do it." Then, if the person asks how he or she can do that, it would be a great time to reply, "Jesus can do that for you. Let me tell you more."

We can trust the Lord to communicate what the dreamer needs to hear. In some cases, He will be hidden. He will also use symbolism that the dreamer will understand once it is pointed out. For instance, if the person dreamt about someone knocking on the front door, and the dreamer was wondering if the door should be opened, that is a biblical symbol. You can say that to the dreamer because God is evoking it in the dream.

If we don't add to the dream, we won't be responsible if

the dreamer doesn't like the interpretation. The person could argue or protest, but he or she will have to interact with God about it because we told the person only what we felt the dream said.

THE FIVE PRIMARY INTERPRETATIVE ENVIRONMENTS: PERSONAL, CHURCH, FAMILY, WORK, OUTREACH

There are five primary environments for dream interpretation. In a *personal* environment, you are developing your interpretation skills for your own use. You have been having dreams, and you are in the lifelong process of developing the skills, understanding, and gifting to move forward in interpretation and know what God is saying to you.

In a *church* environment, the first thing you need to consider is the covering and favor you have there. You will quickly lose the favor of church leadership if you go around interpreting people's dreams without the leadership's knowledge and permission. Find out how they feel about what you want to do and ask for their permission to proceed. They may agree fully, or they may agree as long as it is kept within certain confines. For instance, you may have permission to interpret dreams in a small-group environment or as long as someone else is present, etc. Along with that, dreams can expose a number of potentially sensitive issues, such as strongholds, possible abuse, sin, destiny, moves, births, and other things that require a certain level of favor and maturity on the part of the listener. As you respect these things, you will show church leadership that you are trustworthy.

Interpreting dreams in a *family* environment can be somewhat difficult. You know your children, spouse, parents, siblings, etc., and you have opinions and values concerning them. It can be hard to distinguish between your own understanding and what God is actually saying to the dreamer. On top of that, your loved ones may not take you seriously if the dream deals with an issue the two of you have argued about in the past. For example, your son may have a dream telling him that he needs to be more faithful with his homework. But the odds are you have mentioned this to him before, so if you are the one who gives him the interpretation, you probably won't get the response you would like. In some cases, certain dreams and interpretations are best left with friends or other people who can communicate them more objectively.

Another common place to practice interpretation is at *work*. It is important to be conscious of the language you use there, as well as the time you spend doing non-work-related activities. Certain decisions could have an adverse effect on your long-term career goals.

Many people use their interpretive gifts primarily in *outreach* environments. Usually, you will be the most effective in places where you have some degree of relationship, such as the local coffee shop, bookstore, student union, etc. — wherever you know people and can return on a regular basis. These are the places where you can have the best impact and build relationship and trust.

On the other hand, it is good to be prepared in and out of season as it says in 2 Timothy 4:2, so that you and a friend could go on a walk and end up interpreting dreams for people you meet on the street. You could be at a restaurant, and God opens a door for you to interpret dreams there. Anything is possible.

Venue is very important. I (Zach) have tried just about every sort of venue you can think of, the worst so far being outside a grocery store in a rural town. Before you go somewhere to interpret dreams, consider what people are doing in that venue. At the grocery store, they usually are in a hurry; they are trying not to forget a list that they should have written down. When you ask about interpreting a dream for them, they are thinking, *Was it two pints or a gallon? Was it 2 percent or whole milk?* That is not the ideal time to catch someone.

At the other end of the spectrum, the best venues tend to be cafés, bookshops, pubs, and other zones of leisure. People are there because they don't have to be somewhere else. You can sit and have conversations and speak into their lives. Keep in mind, however, that before you go into any of these places, it is vitally important that you get permission from the management and that you respect what they say. I (Zach) have a really good friend who owns a coffee shop with a mission-related outreach focus. He has seen some powerful transformations occur. But his management also has had to ask people to stop praying, evangelizing, and so on. This is not because they don't want those things — they do. That is their focus. But any type of outreach must be handled with care. People return to the coffee shop because they just love the atmosphere. Picture what would happen if someone suddenly started praying for deliverance over a young girl, and the girl started flopping about on the floor, and the person praying started shouting and rebuking things. How would that affect the

atmosphere? Get permission, or you may lose out on future opportunities and partnerships. We are not saying that loud, disrup-
tive spiritual activity is inherently bad, just that it isn't appropriate
for all situations. We have found that quiet prayer, audible only to
those immediately involved, can be just as effective.

ADDITIONAL INFORMATION ABOUT OUTREACH

As we mentioned, terminology is incredibly important any time
you are interpreting someone's dream. If one of the team members is talking about the *focus* and another member doesn't know
what that means, it can become confusing, and worse, it can look
bad, and be a distraction, to the dreamer. The purpose of the team
is to try to "get out of the way" and let God's message in the
dream come through. With this in mind, when we take teams on
outreach, we usually take only those who have been through our
training programs. This is not to exclude people, but it is an effort
to be as effective as possible with every opportunity that presents
itself.

In addition to respecting the venue and being aware of
language and cultural differences, it is good to go into the environment fully prepared. I (Zach) was preparing to take a dream
interpretation team into a very rowdy, low-end student bar, and
one of the team members wanted to dress up formally. He would
have stuck out very conspicuously and put off our intended audi-
ence. We need to be sensitive to where we are going; otherwise, it
can create a barrier that isn't helpful.

Approach outreach opportunities the way you would a

job interview: Wear appropriate clothing and conduct yourself properly. In general, be neutral — don't do things that are going to interfere with your point of contact. Don't wear a Red Sox hat to an outreach in the Bronx. Be aware of the message your clothing, jewelry, etc. will convey. It is the simple things that are often over-looked, such as remembering to bring breath mints. An *amazing* number of people will eat a dish filled with garlic and onions and then turn up for an outreach without any breath mints. Be sensi-tive and prepared.

Address practical matters. You will need organized ad-ministrators, leaders, team members, people who will pray, people who are good with hospitality, etc. From past experience, I know that it is really wise to have one clear leader. This is the person who handles team interaction and will deal with any difficulties that occur as you go along. As the team leader, it is important to recognize how people work together and be able to balance other considerations such as skill, experience, style, personality, and so on. Try to have a natural mentoring system in place in order to multiply the team.

If your team has members from three different churches, predetermine to which church you should direct dreamers who are interested in learning more. This will help you avoid strife and confusion during the outreach. It is important to note here that outreach events should operate under the authority of a local church.

Also, it is very important to choose your team members well. If you're working with people you find difficult or who don't have the same values you do, you could end up feeling like you're beating your head against a wall. That, obviously, makes it hard to hear from God as you try to interpret someone's dream.

Outreach can be great fun. It is a chance to see the power of God working in people's lives and sometimes see them radically transformed right before your eyes.

YOUR HEART

Whom do you have a heart for? We have mentioned going into New Age festivals, coffee shops, and other venues, but that doesn't mean anyone is confined to those locations. You should find a place where you are naturally relevant. One older person on a team at a coffee shop geared for teenagers is fine, but three fifty-year-old guys talking to a couple of fourteen-year-old girls just looks weird and probably isn't going to end well. Also, if you are a Christian who hasn't had a real friendship with a non-Christian in twenty years, going into a New Age environment and trying to be relevant will be difficult. Start slow and be diligent.

RECORDING THE INTERPRETATION

As a final thought in this section, you might find it helpful to record or make a hardcopy of your interpretation before giving it to the dreamer. This won't always be possible in certain venues, but where feasible, it can be good for a few different reasons. If distractions arise while you are giving the interpretation, you will be able to continue without losing your place.

Second, it helps retain integrity while communicating. If

you get a response from the dreamer that seems negative, it can be tempting to alter or "adjust" the interpretation to avoid conflict. Or if you receive a positive reaction, you may find yourself feeling more confident than you should and exaggerate the nature of the dream. Having a hard copy of the interpretation will help you stay on track.

It is also helpful to have a record so that if the dreamer returns to you later and says, "You said this was going to happen, and it didn't," you can go back and see what you actually said.

CHAPTER 11

EXAMPLES OF THE INTERPRETATION PROCESS

EXAMPLE DREAM:

I dreamt that I was going out a brown door that was leading to no-where in particular. Someone I don't know was coming in the door at the same time, and I knew that I wanted to reach my destination faster than they did. The dream ended as we both seemed to be blocking the other's progress.

1. Focus: The dreamer
Explanation: The dreamer is the focus because without him, there would not be a coherent plot.
2. Sub-focuses: Other person and the door
Explanation: The two most important elements in this dream are the door and the other person

because they are central to the structure of the dream. Brown is important, but it is a detail that adds context to the door.

3. Contextual elements and key details: The brown on the door and a sense of urgency
Explanation: These round out our basic under-standing of what is occurring in the dream. The brown door could speak of compassion or some-thing that is tainted. The dreamer's sense of ur-gency gives the impression that he or she is not in a rush to grow in compassion (the other person's progress is blocked).

Elemental interpretations:
Dreamer = literal
Other person = other people
The door = a new place
Brown = harshness
Personal urgency = self-focused
Nature and scope: internal and metaphoric
Source: God
Category: correction/condition

Interpretation: The dreamer is in a place of transition. This dream is showing that he or she needs to be compassionate toward people who are in different transitions.

EXAMPLE DREAM:

I dreamt I was walking through a church some friends attend in the late afternoon. No one was around, and I was just wandering around. Suddenly, I noticed there were rats among the seats where the choir sits. They were eating crumbs on the floor and gnawing on the church Bibles and hymnals, and they were leaving droppings everywhere.

1. Focus: Church
Explanation: While the dreamer is present and participating, everything he or she is observing relates to something else and not to the dreamer.
2. Sub-focus: Rats, choir area
Explanation: The rats are the primary antagonists in this dream. The choir area gives us a context for their actions.
3. Contextual elements and key details: The Bibles, hymnals, and droppings
Explanation: This is the fruit of what the rats have been up to.

Elemental interpretations:
Church = literal
Rats = negative activity
Choir area = literal? Symbolic of the music team?
Bibles = important symbol
Hymnals = important symbol

Rat droppings = the leftover mess

Nature and scope: external and metaphoric

Source: God

Category: Warning/condition/intercession

Interpretation: This is an external dream that shows the dreamer problems at a friend's church. These are very bad issues and are probably relating to someone or something in the choir area of the church. This is a dream that must be handled very gently and with much prayer and consideration.

EXAMPLE DREAM:

I dreamt that my good friend's wife had a snake that she could control. It was not a threatening snake. But it was with her all the time. People thought it was cool, and she would bring it to parties and make it dance.

1. Focus: Good friend's wife

Explanation: This dream is about the wife's actions.

2. Sub-focus: The snake, people thinking the snake is cool

Explanation: The snake is what the dream is about, but we give the focus to the person who is in control. It is important in the dream that people like the snake because this is not a typical response.

3. Contextual elements and key details: Making the snake dance, parties

Explanation: The dance is a detail concerning the woman who is controlling the snake. Parties show us that the snake is out in the open.

Elemental interpretations:

Good friend's wife = literal

Snake = lies or deception

People thinking the snake is cool = broad deception

Dancing snake = the friend's wife is in control of this deception

Parties = the lie is out in the open but people like it

Nature and scope: external and metaphoric

Source: God

Category: Warning

Interpretation: The dreamer is being made aware that a friend's wife is deceiving a group of people who seem to prefer this to the truth.

EXAMPLE DREAM:

I was wandering the streets of a city looking for something. I didn't know what I was looking for, but I kept seeing "For Rent" signs.

1. Focus: Dreamer

Explanation: The dreamer is driving all the action. He is looking and seeing.

2. Sub-focus: The "For Rent" signs, looking

Explanation: "For Rent" signs are all throughout the dream and provoke a question about their meaning. Looking is what the dreamer spends the whole dream doing.

3. Contextual details and key elements: City, streets

Explanation: The city and the streets are the physical context for the search and therefore should give context to the meaning.

Element interpretations:

Dreamer = literal (this is about the dreamer)

To Let   = toilet (this is a pun)

Looking = seeking something needed

City = the larger area where the dreamer lives

Streets   = outside of known places; streets lead to other places (i.e., not in the dreamer's house, work, or church)

Nature and scope: Internal and metaphoric

Source: God

Category: condition/action

Rough interpretation: You are in a place in life where you are seeking something that you feel you need but aren't sure what it is. This dream is telling you that you need to use a toilet to remove some internal toxins.

Final interpretation: This dream shows that you need a safe place where you can deal with some personal issues, and you haven't found it yet. You have needed this for a while, even though you weren't conscious of it.

EXAMPLE DREAM:

I dreamt that Tom Hanks was going through my attic looking for old underwear. He was wearing a cowboy hat, and I was in charge of holding his laundry basket for him.

> **1. Focus:** Dreamer
> *Explanation:* It is the dreamer's house, underwear, and attic.
> **2. Sub-focus:** Tom Hanks, old underwear
> *Explanation:* Tom Hanks drives the action and provokes strong questions about what he symbolizes. Underwear is the target of the main action.
> **3. Contextual details and key elements:** Cowboy hat, laundry basket, attic, house
> *Explanation:* Each of these provides meaningful context.

Element interpretations:
Dreamer = literal
Tom Hanks = Holy Spirit calling for greater ma-

turity (Thomas can mean "twin"; Jesus said He would send One like Him when He ascended to the Father), need to mature in movie Big, and is cowboy Woody in Toy Story (a story about kids growing up)

Old underwear: old way of being prepared for inner life ("old" and "underwear" have to do with hidden issues and how we handle them)

Attic: storage, things in the brain (attic of body)

Laundry basket: cleaning and maintenance from living and acting

House: life of the dreamer

Nature and scope: internal and metaphoric

Source: God

Category: encouragement/action/condition

Rough interpretation: The dreamer needs to mature and deal with old ways of thinking.

Final interpretation: This dream shows that you are being prompted by the Holy Spirit to evaluate old immature thought processes and renew your mind according to His ways and wisdom.

EXAMPLE DREAM:

I was in my car parked in my parking space. I backed up and hit something. I felt an impact, and then a man on a bicycle circled around my car. I think I hit him, but he didn't act like he had been hit.

1. Focus: Dreamer

Explanation: The dreamer owns the car and causes the main action sequence.

2. Sub-focus: Car, bicycle

Explanation: The action in the dream revolves around the car hitting the bike.

3. Key elements and contextual details: Man, hit, circles, parking space, backing up

Explanation: The man clearly adds context to the bike. Hitting the bike is a key action in the plot, and the parking space and the backing up set context to the other actions.

Element interpretations:

Dreamer = literal

Car = life actions of the dreamer

Bike = personal actions of the man

Man = Son of Man (Jesus)

Backing up = moving backward

Hit = conflict

Parking space = time of inactivity

Circles = reoccurring cycle

Nature and scope: internal and metaphoric

Source: God

Category: understanding/encouragement

Rough interpretation: You are coming out of a time of

spiritual dormancy and trying to get back to what you did before. You seem to be having a hard time relating to Jesus in a personal way, although He is perpetually setting up further opportunities for relationship with you.

Final interpretation: This dream shows that you are coming out of a spiritually inactive season in life and are renewing your personal relationship with Jesus. You think you are messing up, but He is not concerned.

EXAMPLE DREAM:

I was in our home and realized that we had a luxurious "vacation" home that I had forgotten about! How could I forget about that? I felt so privileged to have this home. It seemed to be in a foreign country or perhaps in a style of a foreign country — i.e., a villa. I entered and was looking around the house. It was large, had high ceilings, and was decorated and spacious. It had a feel of luxury. There was a room I knew nothing about. I pushed open the door to find this large dining room. It was furnished with a long, stretched-out table, chairs, etc. I think the walls were painted a burgundy/red, and there was this beautiful, plush, navy blue, cream, and red rug on the floor. There was a beautiful, circular end table that I was considering moving to our current home.

1. Focus: Dreamer
Explanation: The dreamer is the focus of this dream because he or she owns the home and is the beneficiary of its existence and features.

2. Sub-focus: Vacation home

Explanation: The vacation home is a sub-focus because it structurally holds the plot of the dream together.

3. Contextual elements and key details: foreign country, dining room, luxury, red, blue

Explanation: These elements all bring context to understanding what is in the dream. The foreign country is out of context to the house because that is where it is located. The dining room focuses on a specific area inside the house. Luxury adds to the nature of the house, and the colors typically indicate specific manifestations of the Holy Spirit.

Element interpretations:

Dreamer = literal

Vacation house = spiritual life of peace (houses often represent the lives of those who live in them, and the fact that it is a vacation home talks about rest and peace)

Foreign = heavenly (foreign means not known, and in this case, a "house not known" refers to Heaven as a different land than this one)

Dining room = spiritual food and fellowship (the room where you eat with others)

Luxury = extravagance (this is a fairly literal meaning of something above and beyond basic need or provision)

Red = wisdom (based on Isaiah 11:2 and the rainbow)

Blue = knowledge of God (also based on Isaiah 11:2 and the rainbow)

Nature and scope: internal and metaphoric

Source: God

Category: knowledge/calling

Rough interpretation: You have been forgetting your eternal heavenly life while living your earthly one. There is peace, rest, and abundance for you. There is spiritual activity for you that you don't even know about yet. This unknown activity is comprised of great provision coming through rest and relationship.

Final interpretation: This dream is an invitation to remember your eternal life in Heaven and bring it into your daily life. God has abundant peace and rest for you. You are being shown a deeper level of fellowship with Him than you have ever experienced, and you are being called to prepare for it in your life.

CHAPTER 12

COMMON DREAMS

There are certain types of dreams, or pieces of dreams, that often come up as we do dream interpretations. Now that you are familiar with the *elements* commonly found in dreams, knowing these common dreams and their meanings should cause a light to go on for you. You have probably had a lot of these dreams yourself.

God gives dreams and they have meaning, and there are some "common" dreams that often fit a common framework. If you can interpret the more common dreams, you will have a good foundation for interpreting the potentially more difficult, less common dreams.

NAKED DREAMS

Almost everyone has had at least one naked dream. We don't

mean a sexual dream; we mean being naked in an abnormal environment. There could be other meanings, but the most common definition for naked dreams concerns vulnerability. Naked dreams often leave people feeling confused or embarrassed, but actually, nakedness is the purest form of vulnerability that humans can experience.

Naked dreams can be good or bad. You could dream that you're with a group of people, and everyone but you is fully clothed. In most cases, that would mean you are being transparent with them, and they are not necessarily being transparent with you. Or you could have a naked dream showing you that you have no covering, no protection, and you're fully exposed. In that case, it could be implying a lack of emotional or relational safety. The context of the dream should show you what is what.

BATHROOM DREAMS

There is a wide range of bathroom dreams, from showering to using the toilet. At times, they can be graphic and messy, and they may make you think that God has no discretion! But bathroom dreams often have to do with being clean or internally processing things that you need to get rid of, such as relational, social, or emotional issues. Dreaming about going to the toilet, for instance, could represent removing the toxins from within you.

A showering dream is a similar idea, but it would deal more specifically with impurities outside the body. When you wash your hands or take a shower, you're cleansing the outside, but when you're using the toilet, you're getting rid of toxins, or processing things, on the inside.

Related to that, if you dream about a bathroom that is overflowing, filthy, or just not kept up well, it could mean that the place or situation in which you're cleansing yourself isn't up to par, or as clean, neat, or maintained as it should be.

Again, it is always important to look at the context when you are interpreting a dream. If you are showering in front of a large group of colleagues, that would potentially denote a public process going on in front of your peers, whereas if you are showering privately in the normal context, that would denote a cleansing process going on in private.

TEETH OR HAIR LOSS/FAILING EYESIGHT DREAMS

With all three of these types, it is important to know what the individual elements mean.

Eyes would represent vision and a sense of where you're going. Teeth represent wisdom and your ability to cope with or process things (you "chew" on something in order to understand it). Hair represents your glory and your covering (1 Corinthians 11:15). If those things are falling out, failing, or deteriorating, it often relates to something going on within the dream that will let you know what attack or difficulty you are facing. If you dream you're at the office, and you suddenly start losing your teeth, that likely means you're unsure about something related to your vocation, immediate employment, or current project. If you dream that you're driving a car and you're having more and more trouble seeing the road in front of you, it may mean that you don't have vision for where you're going or what you're involved in.

I (Jim) remember doing a dream outreach at Virginia Tech, and this guy who looked bored and like he didn't want to be there said, "Here is a dream. I had a dream where my teeth were falling out."

We were doing this outreach at a school, and I felt that the dream meant he didn't really understand what he was studying. That was the basic interpretation I gave him, and it impacted him so much that he came back with his friends.

Remember that context is always important. You shouldn't interpret all similar dreams the same way because each dreamer is going through different things in his or her life. I remember doing another interpretation event in a related venue, and a woman shared a similar dream, one in which she was losing her teeth. In that instance, however, I felt the dream wasn't about what she was studying; it felt more that she didn't understand what was going on in her life. That interpretation impacted her as well.

EX-GIRLFRIEND/EX-BOYFRIEND DREAMS

Dreams about exes can be confusing. Keep in mind that if God uses an ex in your dream, He isn't necessarily saying, "This person was right in the relationship, and you were wrong." He is simply using that symbol because it is very powerful. As He uses it, it will heal and uncover issues in your life concerning Him as well as that person. He will redeem symbols by using them.

Dreams about exes are very common. If you are dreaming of your first boyfriend or girlfriend, it could be an issue of your first love: that is, God and His position in your heart. Similarly, this type of dream could also represent an old love: something you used to have affection for that is coming back into your life, either good or bad. It could be something that you got rid of that is trying to creep back in. It will take discernment and understanding of the context to determine which it is.

There may also be times when God uses your ex to represent Himself even if your history with that person is negative. For instance, it may be that your ex-husband is the only metaphor readily available to represent the groom, or your ex-wife may be the only metaphor available to represent the bride of Christ. Again, He may be stirring up your issues with your ex because He wants to heal relational problems between you and Him. It could be the *role* of the person that God is using.

Finally, dreaming about exes can sometimes represent past seasons of your life. They can take you back to wherever you were mentally, emotionally, and spiritually at the time of that relationship and bring up the things you were dealing with. I (Zach) remember doing a dream outreach where a girl came up to me with a dream she wanted interpreted. She was engaged and very happy, but she'd had this dream about an ex-boyfriend who was trying to get back together with her. It had been a difficult, abusive relationship in real life, and she was considering leaving the good relationship she was in to go back to the previous relationship, because she assumed the dream meant she still had feelings for him. But that was not what the dream was saying. I felt that the dream was essentially a soul dream. She was picking up on her ex's desire to restart a relationship with her.

Don't assume that dreaming about an ex means you're supposed to get back with the person. Most likely, it will *not* mean that.

DREAMING ABOUT DEAD FRIENDS AND RELATIVES

This is a difficult type of dream to deal with because of the number of people you'll meet who dreamt about their friend dying, and a week later, the person actually did die. It can produce a large amount of guilt or even shame, and the dreamers often feel like they didn't do enough, or that they didn't do what needed to be done. Those situations can be difficult to go through.

However, most of the time when people dream about dead relatives or people dying, it is metaphoric in nature. It often speaks of a loss of influence with that particular person or whatever the person represents. The dream may deal with the person's name, nature, personality, or the role that he or she had in the dreamer's life while alive. The dream may be metaphorically using who that person is or was.

A dead person could also represent a dead issue or something that has ended, either good or bad. It could represent the end of a season.

Additionally, keep in mind that Christians who are alive with Jesus may have a role that goes beyond their physical life spans. As previously mentioned, the Bible talks about the great cloud of witnesses: people of faith who surround us and observe our activities on Earth (Hebrews 12:1–2). As they are witnesses, God may send them to "witness" to us about something of Him.

They are interacting with Him, and He may use them in dreams to convey messages in an almost angelic way.

FLYING DREAMS

There are various types of flying dreams: flying from place to place, trying to fly, floating, etc. Flying is highly evocative of spiritual activity. Usually, if flying is a conscious decision on your part (you weren't flying and then you realized you could fly), it is often an indication that you're lucid dreaming: You're *aware* in the dream, and your spirit is ruling.

If you have a dream about flying over buildings, trees, or other elements, it essentially means that you are ascending over issues that would try to keep you down. You are spiritually overcoming. Your spirit is bringing you up, and you are not being conquered by anything that is not of God.

Flying in dreams can also denote a season of victory in your life.

FALLING DREAMS

Falling dreams are usually about insecurity or feeling ungrounded. Your feet are not underneath you, in both a physical and metaphorical sense. I (Zach) don't know that I've ever talked with a pregnant woman who hasn't had a dream about falling. During pregnancy, the physical and emotional changes occurring can produce a sense of insecurity, and dreams will often reflect what a person is feeling, consciously or subconsciously.

Look at the context for more information, such as what is causing the falling or what you are falling toward or away from. These can help you understand what type of insecurity the dream is highlighting and potentially how to address it.

Control can also be a root cause of falling dreams: You feel out of control, things are out of control, or you're dealing with control issues.

Falling dreams don't necessarily mean that you are literally about to experience some type of fall in your life. They could simply be addressing how you feel. Contrary to popular belief, we have never spoken with people who dreamt they were falling and then woke up dead!

DREAMS OF BEING CHASED

This type of dream typically reveals issues of fear. The specific issues could be addressed within the dream: You are literally being chased by something, your real-life fears are being manifested, or you are terrified that something is after you.

In many dreams like these, you can't get away from what is chasing you; it is like you are moving in slow motion. This usually means that you are not facing your fears. Instead, you are running, or trying to run, and the issue is not being addressed. Depending on what that issue is, these dreams will often stop when you decide not to run from it in real life. If it is a recurring dream, it will probably keep recurring until you choose to face the thing you fear.

Sometimes, the dream contains a means in which to conquer the thing that is after you. I (Zach) remember talking with a man who had been having a recurring dream for weeks about being chased by this large, scary creature. On a whim, I asked him if anybody else was there with him in the dream.

He said, "You know, yes. I was running around and around this rock, and up on top of it was Gandalf the White. He was just kind of sitting there."

"Next time," I said, "do you think you could ask him to help you?"

Understanding began to dawn. "Yeah, that's probably why he was there."

Children experience chasing dreams fairly often. They usually have to do with the enemy testing or attacking their call to lead, so that as they grow up, they learn in their dreams that they will be pursued or injured if they are who God has called them to be.

DREAMS ABOUT BEING LOST, TRAPPED, OR LOSING SOMETHING

This is a broad category, and it is especially important to look at context. Very often, being lost in a dream signifies a lack of direction, either physically or spiritually. It may be God correcting you; perhaps you think you are going down the right path, but you should be doing something else instead. This type of dream is often meant to draw you to a place of being closer to God and seeking Him.

The trap metaphor could be somewhat literal in that you

are feeling trapped, or there is a trap that has been set in your way. If you are feeling trapped, something in real life is probably causing you to feel that way. Conversely, if it is an actual trap, the dream is showing you something you're not aware of: a trap that has been hidden from you.

Similar to dreams in which you are losing your hair or teeth, being lost in a dream can mean that you feel lost and don't know who you are, where you're going, or what you're looking for. The dream could have a lot of emotional connotation, or it could simply be saying, "You don't know what you're doing. You're lost, and you need to figure out where you're going."

Again, context and emotion will tell you a lot in dreams such as these. If you are lost but don't feel lost, there may be some areas in life where you are off track. Being lost and feeling panicked about it indicates that you may feel lost in real life, and you know it.

Similarly, people often dream about losing something valuable. Losing a possession in a dream can tell you that something of yours, or something you care about, is no longer with you. The lost item could vary widely. For example, if you lose your driver's license in the dream, it could be an indication that you are losing a sense of who you are.

Keep in mind that there is a substantial difference between *feeling* lost and actually *being* lost. The dream could be telling you, "You feel this way," and not, "You are this way." You could *feel* you're lost more than you actually are lost. So you have to use discernment, consider context, and not jump to conclusions.

The dream's meaning really depends on what is being

lost, whether or not you care about it, etc. For instance, if you are losing weight in a dream, it could be positive in the sense that you're losing excess baggage. If you're losing something that you're better off not having, God could be showing you that He is removing things you don't need.

Also, losing possessions can help us realize the value we place on things. The plot of the dream can be a process that teaches us something we need to know. I (Zach) remember having a dream in high school about losing my car. It ceased to exist. The dream worked through how I related to that freedom and how that freedom was such an important part of my identity. The result was that I was able to realign how I approached certain possessions.

BACK-IN-SCHOOL DREAMS

There are two things commonly involved with back-in-school dreams. Historically speaking, we know that we will face the same test again and again if we don't pass it the first time, and there are certain issues we need to stay on top of. So if you dream about being back at school and possibly taking a test, the dream could be letting you know that you are dealing with an issue you have dealt with before, and you need to be alert concerning it. If you passed the test last time, this could be a slightly harder test. If you failed the test last time, you probably need to be more careful or attentive this time.

In a typical back-in-school dream that deals with recurring issues, the context of the dream will feel "old school." For instance, you could be younger in the dream, or it is the same school you attended as a kid or young adult. That could indicate the dream is dealing with issues that have come up in the past.

If you dream that you're at some other school or taking a test you know you haven't taken before, the dream could be indicating that you are being schooled or tested in something. It may not have to do with the past if there isn't a lot of previous context involved or "school feelings." Do you feel like you're back at school in the dream, or do you feel like you're just at school and taking a test? That will shade the interpretation.

TELEPHONE DREAMS

Another common dream involves telephones, particularly ones that aren't working. You could dream that your phone is broken, the call won't go through, etc. This could be indicative of communication issues or your feeling that God isn't listening to your prayers.

Who you are calling, or who is trying to call you, could also show you what the dream is about. If you get a call and answer it, but you can't hear the person on the other end, it could be that you know God is speaking to you, but you don't know what He is saying.

Or if you have a phone that you know is broken, it could be that there is an issue going on with your *calling*. That sort of dream is more of a pun, and the rest of the dream should help you discern that.

Finally, dreams about broken phones can represent feelings of isolation; perhaps you are feeling like you don't have anyone you can truly communicate with. In some cases, you may have dreams where the phone doesn't work, but then you realize how to make it work. That could indicate that you are discovering how to pull yourself out of isolation or away from the difficulty you are having.

DROWNING OR CHOKING DREAMS

If you dreamt that you were drowning, it could indicate that you feel "in over your head," or that you feel pressed down or smothered. Dreams like these could also indicate that you're in a spiritual environment where the atmosphere isn't good for you.

Related to drowning dreams, choking dreams show that you are being attacked and, typically, that the enemy is trying to cut off your ability to breathe by the Spirit. In Genesis, God breathed the Spirit into us and gave us life, so choking could reveal an attack that is coming against an ability to function in who God is — that is, to minister in and be sustained by the Spirit.

TRAVELING DREAMS

Traveling dreams are often about gaining a new perspective on a situation. Where you end up in the dream could be very important and revealing. If you're on a vacation, the dream could be about getting away and seeing new things. If you're traveling to a new location (that is, you are moving), it can be indicative of a change in your life.

Even though it may use a geographic metaphor, the dream could be speaking of moving toward your destiny, moving on, or changing in some other way. The context will tell you a lot. Is the travel permanent, such as a geographical move? Or is it temporary? Are you looking forward to it? All these things will help show you what type of change is going on in your life.

STORM DREAMS

Frequently, people will dream about storms. Tornados, hurricanes, snowstorms, hailstorms, earthquakes, tsunamis, other geographical events — all of these can represent a coming attack or a destructive force. Conversely, they could also represent a change or a movement that is of God and powerfully affecting everything around it. You could have more than one of these storms in the same dream, or you may have dreams that are about just one dramatic event.

All geographical events in dreams could be of God. They could be times of trial, great seasons of attack, and the like. Often, the tone or coloration of the storm, or your feelings about it, will help you discern the source of the storm and what is going on. You could dream about a storm and know that trouble is coming, or you could dream about it and think, *This is awesome!* In the latter case, the finger of God could be touching things in a traumatic way, but it is still God.

These elements are not called "acts of God" for nothing. One of the things often misunderstood in dreams like these is the level of power involved. If the storm is incredibly powerful, dreamers will often give it a sinister meaning, when God is quite power-ful, and it could be representative of His power. Devastation often seems absolutely terrifying, but there are times when it is actually cleansing. For example, you could dream that a huge tornado or hurricane comes and cleans the countryside; it removes the things that weren't meant to be there. Depending on the context, that is destructive but not necessarily sinister.

CAR TROUBLE DREAMS

Car troubles in dreams often signify things related to your voca-tion, calling, or mode of operation. You may or may not know about these difficulties in real life. For instance, if your brakes fail in your dream, it may mean you have lost the ability to keep your-self under control. If the battery is dead, it may mean you have run yourself ragged.

Pay attention to the *type* of the automobile in your dream. Is it a pick-up truck or a sedan? Look at the size and also who is in it. That will tell you the scope of the dream and give you a great context clue. If you are in a bus with everyone from work, the dream is probably about work and what everyone at work is doing: the combined vocational activity that everyone is involved in. If you are in a car with your bowling team, it is probably about what you're doing with the team or what the team represents. If you are with people from your church, it would indicate the activ-ity or ministry going on in the church.

Vocational vehicles will give you another great clue about the meaning of the dream. If you are in a plumber's truck, you're probably dealing with a *leaking* issue, whether it is an emotional leak or something relational in nature.

SNAKE DREAMS

This is one of the most common dreams people will talk about and be bothered about. From a biblical perspective, snakes typically have to do with deception or lies.

One of the first dreams I (Jim) interpreted came up while I was working at a bank. A coworker who didn't know I studied dreams told me that she dreamt her mother-in-law was throwing white snakes at her. My coworker was cutting the heads off and being splattered with blood. When I told her that the dream said her mother-in-law was telling white lies about her (things that aren't inherently very harmful but can cause emotional heartache), she almost fell over. The truth resounded with her. In that instance, white snakes represented white lies. If you dream about handing out huge black snakes to people, that would show a much clearer deception going on.

If snakes are chasing you, it could mean that other people's deception or deceit is trying to get you. If a snake is simply present in your dream and it isn't attacking you, it can mean there is some deceit that is "sticking around" until it is dealt with.

In 99.99 percent of dreams, snakes aren't good. They usually represent an untruth or something that isn't trustworthy. But there are *some* cases in which snakes are good. The Bible says to be as wise as a serpent, so your dream could be talking about wisdom. In most cases, however, it won't be, so really examine the dream and be sure you're not trying to be nice to yourself or to someone else by saying the dream doesn't mean deception.

As you move forward in interpreting dreams, it is good to remember that most dreams are about stuff that is going on around you. When you have a dream about snakes, you need to be honest about your own issues and the situations you're involved in so that if this is an issue with someone else, you've been diligent to check your own heart first.

DREAMS ABOUT DOGS

Traditionally, dogs have been called man's best friend. That being the case, dreams about dogs are often about close friendships — very faithful and loyal relationships. (Puppies are "small dogs" and could represent children.)

Dogs can also represent fears, based on how the dreamer feels about them. If you love dogs, the dog is probably positive. If you are afraid of them, it could have a negative meaning. When you are interpreting someone else's dream about a dog, it is important to find out how the dreamer feels about them. Deal with context in the dream and context in the person's life.

Dogs are one of those elements that dreamers will often understand better than interpreters will because they know how they feel about the animal. I (Jim) have been in some situations in which I have known what the entire dream meant — except for the little white poodle. But then the dreamer says, "That's the only thing I knew the meaning of. When I was a kid, I always held my little poodle when I was scared, and she made me feel safe." We have all sorts of different relationships with our animals, so the dreamer is often in the best place to understand what that specific animal meant in the dream.

HOUSE DREAMS

In many house dreams, the house isn't the main element of the dream; other elements and activities are more prominent, but the dream takes place in the house.

Houses typically represent your life. We talked about cars representing vocational activities and things you are doing. Similarly, houses represent where you live. The context is important, as well as the size of the house and who is in it: The house will typically represent the life issues of those people.

It can also be important to note who owns the house, whether it is your house specifically or if it is someone else's. The dream could be telling you how you relate to or understand someone. If the dream takes place in your own house, and all your family and extended family are present, the dream would likely be about the living issues in your bloodline.

The room you are in can give you even more context. If you are in the living room, these are *living* issues. If you are in the kitchen, these may be issues of how you're being sustained and fed.

SEX DREAMS

Dreams involving sex often make people quite uncomfortable, but the truth is that many sex dreams are simply about intimacy.

There are two types of sexual dreams: dreams involving sex and pornographic dreams. You deal with the two in very different ways. Typically, dreams about sex and other forms of intimacy across the board are about relationship and covenant, whereas dreams dealing with pornographic or lust issues will have a much more sexual feel to them.

It is not uncommon for people to have dreams about being intimate with someone other than their spouses. They wake up feeling that they are being unfaithful, when the dream is really about intimacy with God. My wife (Jim) had a dream where she was in a hospital bed, and the doctor was really good looking. She knew she was in love with him, but she felt awful because she is married to me. She woke up feeling terrible and thinking she had adultery in her heart. But the moment she told me her dream, I knew it had been about the Great Physician. The dream wasn't telling her she was being unfaithful at all; it was about how much she loves the Lord.

You could have dreams about intimacy with God that may *imply* there was sex, but they won't be graphic. In some cases, your sensibilities may be offended. Be aware of them when you're trying to determine if the dream was about intimacy or if it was pornographic in nature. You might have so much guilt that you quickly assume it was the latter, but use in-dream context and not your real-life response. Your general feeling about sex may cause you to think it is something that it isn't.

MISSING TRANSPORTATION DREAMS

Many people dream about missing a bus, a plane, a car ride, etc. Dreams like these can be similar to falling dreams in that you aren't or don't feel prepared, or aren't in the right place at the right time. The dream could be letting you know that you feel insecure about something or that something is coming against you. It could also be a warning dream, letting you know that you are in danger of missing an opportunity or that you did miss an opportunity, which could be good or bad depending on the context.

WORK DREAMS

Dreams about work could address your job or vocational choices; they could be about things that *parallel* work, such as being under authority or doing what you have been called to do. They could also have a larger purpose and signify what you are doing on this earth that exists outside your work situation.

Dreams about transition or changes in your job can let you know what is about to happen in real life. You could dream that you are at work and suddenly the environment changes. This could be a dream showing you how to approach certain situations and perhaps telling you to take opportunities as they come along.

RECURRING DREAMS

One of the keys with common dreams is that they often recur in certain seasons of our lives. They usually have to do with on-going issues or messages. If you have been having the same dream for the last ten years, it could be that your situation isn't changing or that God is trying to send you a message that requires a response.

For me (Jim), it isn't uncommon to talk to people about recurring dreams they had for years that stopped when the dreamers moved from their house or apartment to another location. In those cases, the dreams were probably being caused by something in their environment. If they had recurring dreams about weird, creepy sexual things while they were living in a certain apartment, it is likely that weird, creepy sexual things were going on in that building or neighborhood, or had gone on with previous residents. When the dreamers then moved to a different house or apartment, the dreams stopped because the weird sexual things weren't in their family; the dreamers were picking up on activities going on around them, not within them.

Recurring dreams could also be about things that need your attention. Any issue you're not dealing with or responding to could keep coming up in your dream life. For example, God may want you to apologize for something, and until you do, you may have a recurring dream that shows you the steps you should take. You could also have recurring dreams about an illness you're dealing with, how you feel about God, how you are coping with your environment, etc. Some of those dreams will continue until the condition changes or you are able to leave that situation.

SUMMARY

In this chapter, we covered common interpretations for common dreams. These are *pieces* of dreams that we have regularly come across as we interpret our own dreams and talk to others about theirs. Obviously, when interpreting any aspect of any dream, context is really important. Many things could vary the definitions we have mentioned here depending on the context.

Keep in mind that there are other interpretations for these elements that are less common, and this book does not discuss those. If you had a dream that didn't seem to mean what we talked about here, don't feel that you have to change the interpretation God has given you to match what we said. You aren't necessarily doing something wrong if your interpretations don't match these common ones. In some cases, we could give you another ten or twenty options for what these dreams could mean in different contexts. This chapter covered only the more common meanings. Whenever we discuss the common meanings of elements and different types of dreams, it is meant to jumpstart you and get the metaphoric thought flowing within you, as well as help you with the backlog of dreams you may have.

This book is not meant to be exhaustive. It is meant to be a starting point and reference guide. The moment you take the list of elements and examples that we have included here, try to use it as the rules and laws of dream interpretation, and stop thinking and discerning, you will find that the list becomes completely ineffective. In a way, it only works when you *don't* rely on it. Why is that? Because dream interpretation is an invitation to draw nearer to God. Knowing what something could mean *increases* your need for discernment; it doesn't decrease it. Being informed, educated, and discerning can give you a good start on dealing with common meanings or eliminating them quickly.

Discernment is always important. Knowing the common interpretation allows you to hold it up to a dream and use your discernment to see if there is a match — if that is what the metaphor means in that specific instance. Spiritual discernment will say, "No, it is different," or, "Yes, it is similar." Both of those answers are helpful. If you know the common meaning is not what the element means in your dream, you know you can go in a different direction. Maybe it is a pun instead, or there are important contextual clues you are missing. But if it is similar, you don't have to take it word for word. Instead, you can ask, "How is it similar? How do I deal with it in this specific situation?"

If you do what we suggest in this book, keep your heart open, and practice your discernment, you will find yourself on a firm and steady road to knowing what your dreams mean.

CHAPTER 13

THE IMPORTANCE
OF CHARACTER
IN DREAM INTERPRETATION

A s our interest in dreams is first realized, we are often like little kids with a new toy. There is so much joy and excitement. *Oh, my goodness! I never realized God speaks to me like this.* Dreams can be life changing. However, they affect us positively only when God is kept at the center of our pursuit of them. Dreams are one small aspect of our Christian faith. We should be able to look at them, recognize their significance, know how to apply them, and remain productive members of our church and society. As with all forms of receiving revelation, dreams should not be elevated to the extent that nothing else is ever discussed or considered important.

We look for certain signs of "dream maturity" as we teach on this topic. Can the dreamer communicate the dream with others in a wholesome way that is clear and understandable? Is the dreamer moving forward in his or her relationship with God? The result of any growth in God is growth in character that can be measured by godly fruit. This is noticeably true with dream interpretation. In fact, the better you get at dream interpretation, the more you will realize that if there is any limit to your gifting, it is your character — in this case, as it pertains to sensitivity and reliance on God. You may have the skill, the ability, the anointing, and everything you need to interpret that dream, but then you run into a stronghold in your own life that won't allow you to progress.

Any issue within you that isn't in alignment with God could and likely will cause a problem as you try to interpret your dreams. It will stop you from being able to hear from God completely or accurately in that particular area. For instance, if you have unforgiveness in your heart and are not willing to deal with it, you will likely have a hard time interpreting any dream that addresses that topic. You will find yourself hitting blocks and discovering problems with your interpretations that you won't immediately be able to understand or resolve. Character issues come up in dreams constantly, and any obstacles, strongholds, or other topics we are trying to avoid will *certainly* come up. They are blind spots in our lives that prevent us from seeing what is truly going on. So they affect the way we interpret our own dreams, and they also affect the way we interpret others' dreams. If we can't see clearly for ourselves, we won't be able to see clearly for people we are trying to help or mentor.

We need character for character's sake, but as this is a book about dreams, we want to emphasize the importance of character as a means of being able to hear God's voice. Godly character keeps us humble and teachable; it allows us to walk in His discernment and interpret metaphors much more accurately. Many revelatory pictures or dreams can be "fit" to mean what we want them to mean rather than what God is actually saying. Character helps us address what needs to be addressed and be open to God's voice, no matter what He chooses to reveal to us. It is a preference for growth, rather than assuming we are in an ideal place and do not need to change.

Godly character also keeps us from mixing opinions or advice into interpretations or representing God flippantly, unconcerned with whether or not our words are accurate or how they will affect the dreamer. When people come across interpreters who are irreverent or frivolous with the meaning of their dreams, they will be "turned off" from that particular interpreter, from dreams as a whole, or possibly even from God.

I (Zach) was on an outreach a few years ago, and one of the team members ended up having to be removed because he had a certain harshness when he was speaking to people. It just wasn't acceptable. A young woman came to me on the verge of tears after having her dream interpreted. All her friends had had these fantastic, really amazing interpretations, but she had gone away feeling like she had been lied to because this certain interpreter had changed the interpretation so it would align with what he wanted to say. She could tell that the interpretation didn't match the dream.

All this being said, we need to be people who are willing to recognize when we are wrong and be willing to change. Those are excellent signs that we are reasonably healthy and on the way to maturity. When we interpret dreams, we should be open to hearing we were mistaken, and we should seek to know how we could do it better next time. Humility is so important.

We don't know a single dream interpreter who started as an expert. Instead, you start as someone who is hungry for God and perhaps has some calling and gifting but needs training in it. At times, that training comes from people who are better or more experienced, and sometimes it comes from people who will tell you, "I don't know what you're doing wrong, but your interpretation is not quite right. You need to go search out the answer." If your motivation is godly and you want to know what God is saying and doing, you'll take any correction you can get. You will be the wise man Solomon described in **Proverbs 9:8**: "Reprove a wise man and he will love you." Trying to be perfect or prove you have a gift is *hard* work. It is much more difficult trying to maintain that delusion than to admit you need some help.

IN CONCLUSION

It all comes down to this: When you go to interpret dreams, be like Jesus. All the things He taught and modeled about life, having character and integrity, and being kind, loving, and gentle are very relevant with dreams.

Dream interpretation is not a gift that opts you out of character growth, humility, correction, accountability, relationship, and being loving and teachable. It is like the rest of your walk; you need to do it with fear and trembling (Philippians 2:12). We should approach dream interpretation with a deep awe and fear of God. Dreams are *powerful*, and so their interpretations must be treated with respect, whether we are interpreting our own dreams or helping other dreamers with theirs.

We briefly mentioned in Chapter Ten the priestly role that coincides with dream interpreters. When we help people with their dreams, we are stepping into a role that is similar to the priest's role in the peace offering described in Leviticus 3–4. The point of the sacrifice was to be at peace with God. When people have dreams from God that they don't understand, one reason they seek the interpretation is so that they will have resolution — so they will have peace. We help them in this so they will be able to cooperate with Him. That is a serious thing. When interpreters don't do that and see dreams just as a platform to show others they are gifted or to advance their own ministry, the people they have been called to help will eventually see through that and will probably begin to look for someone else they can trust.

Interpreting dreams is a lifelong process of growing in the language of God, in the knowledge of His ways, in humility and trust, and also in the area of *searching out* the mysteries He hides for you (Proverbs 25:2). Some dreams will be hard for you to interpret because the journey of learning to interpret them will cause you to know God in ways that you wouldn't have if you hadn't tried. When you have interpreted that dream, not only will you know what the dream means, but you will know God in a way you didn't before.

Dreams that are steeped with mystery spur us toward growth, so as you get better at interpreting dreams at a certain level, God will start sending you dreams that are harder. It isn't that He is getting more mysterious or cryptic, but He is exposing you to more and more of His nature, and that nature in its infinite variability is something that seems strange to us as we come in contact with it. God wants to be known by us, and He will release more of His ways and His nature as we "unwrap" the previous ways.

In other words, as we get better at interpreting dreams, we can expect the mystery of dreaming and the ways of God to get bigger, not smaller. You may find yourself feeling that you know less about Him now than you did when you started, because now you are more aware of aspects of Him that you don't yet understand. This is a good thing. It means that He will always be bigger than you, and there will always be more of Him to explore.

This is the journey you are on as you learn to interpret dreams. It is a journey of encountering the unbelievable hugeness of God — not just how powerful, all loving, all knowing, and wise He is, but just how many different facets He has that we have not yet seen and that He wants to make known to us.

You have begun a journey of knowing God and His ways that will continue through all eternity. Dream interpretation is not something you read about once and then you're an expert. You begin the journey, and if you persevere, it never ends.

GLOSSARY OF TERMS

Context: The dream's environment or oddities that help us understand the elements.

Dissect: To pick important elements out of a dream and place them into some form of list or graph.

Dream category: A way of looking at a dream that helps bring some understanding to the purpose or intent of the dream.

Dream classification: One of four groups that various dream categories fit into.

Dream cycle: The process that a person goes through starting with preparing a dream and ending with the fulfillment of the dream. You can be in the midst of many dream cycles at any given time.

Dream interpretation team: Two or more people working together to interpret dreams.

Dream outreach: Two or more dream interpreters actively seeking dreams to interpret.

Dream scenes: The pieces of a dream after it has been broken down into multiple parts where the dream environment changes.

Elements: Items within a dream that add context or meaning to the dream.

External nature: A dream that has application relating to something outside the dreamer.

Final interpretation: A smooth, clear interpretation that conveys the meaning of the dream and can be given to the dreamer.

Focus: Who or what the dream is about.

Internal nature: A dream that has personal application.

Interpret: To bring understanding.

Interpretive framework: The step-by-step process for interpreting dreams.

Key details: Dream elements that are not a focus or sub-focus but seem important.

Metaphor: Something that represents something else.

Nature: Determines if the application of the dream is internal or external.

Rough interpretation: The first interpretation of a dream that needs to be "edited" before it is relayed to the dreamer.

Scope: Determines if a dream or element is literal or metaphoric.

Sub-focus: Very important parts or elements of a dream that contribute to understanding the focus.

Summarize: Recounting a dream in such a way that it is manageable, without leaving out any important or key parts.

BIBLIOGRAPHY

Benner, Jeff A. *The Ancient Hebrew Language and Alphabet: Understanding the Ancient Hebrew Language of the Bible Based on Ancient Hebrew Culture and Thought.* Virtualbookworm.com Publishing, 2004.

Cave, William. *The History of the Lives, Acts, Death, and Martyrdoms of Those Who Were Contemporary with, or Immediately Succeeded, the Apostles; As Also the Most Eminent of the Primitive Fathers for the First Three Hundred Years.* Philadelphia, PA: Solomon Wiatt, 1810. Page 237.

Gnuse, Robert Karl. *Dreams and Dream Reports in the Writings of Josephus: A Traditio-Historical Analysis.* Leiden, the Netherlands: Brill Academic Publishers, 1996. Page 7.

Kelsey, Morton T. *God, Dreams, and Revelation: A Christian Interpretation of Dreams.* Minneapolis, MN: Augsburg, 1991. Page 104.

Osborn, Eric Francis. *Justin Martyr.* Tuebingen, Germany: Mohr Siebeck, 1973.

Savary, Louis M.; Berne, Patricia H.; Williams, Strephon Kaplan. *Dreams and Spiritual Growth: A Judeo-Christian Way of Dreamwork.* Mahwah, NJ: Paulist Press, 1984. Page 39.

Irenaeus, *The Treatise of Irenæus of Lugdunum Against the Heresies (v.2): A Translation of the Principal Passages, With Notes and Arguments.* General Books LLC. 2010 Reprint.

Miller, Patricia Cox. *Dreams in Late Antiquity: Studies in the Imagination of a Culture.* Princeton, NJ: Princeton University Press, 1994. Pages 93–94.

Robertson, James Craigie. *History of the Christian Church to the Pontificate of Gregory the Great, A.D. 590.*

Bulkeley, Kelly. *Visions of the Night: Dreams, Religion, and Psychology*. Albany, NY: State University of New York Press, 1999.

Krippner, Stanley, et al. *Extraordinary Dreams and How to Work with Them*. Albany: State University of New York Press, 2002. Page 24.

Lamon, Ward Hill. *Recollections of Abraham Lincoln*. Lincoln, NE: University of Nebraska Press, 1994. Page 113.

Bear, Mark F., et al. *Neuroscience: Exploring the Brain*. Lippincott Williams & Willkins, 2006. Page 103.

Spignesi, Stephen J.; Lewis, Michael. *Here, There, and Everywhere: The 100 Best Beatles Songs*. Black Dog & Leventhal Publishers, 2004 reprint.

Cryer, Max. *Love Me Tender: The Stories Behind the World's Best-loved Songs*. London: Frances Lincoln, 2008. Page 57.

Hamp, David. *Discovering the language of Jesus: Hebrew or Aramaic?* CreateSpace, 2005.

Strong, James. *The New Strong's Expanded Exhaustive Concordance of the Bible*. Nashville, TN: Thomas Nelson, 2010.

Bronson, Po; Merryman, Ashley. *Nuture Shock*. New York: Twelve. 2009.

Holt, Robert H. *Psychoanalysis and Contemporary Science*. London: Collier-Mac-Millian, 1973.

Hall, James Albert. *Jungian Dream Interpretation*. Toronto: Inner City Books. 1983.

Klingberg, Torkel. *The Overflowing Brain: Information Overload and the Limits of Working Memory.* Oxford University Press, 2009.

Vedfelt, Ole. (Attributed to Freud.) *The Dimensions of Dreams: The Nature, Function, and Interpretation of Dreams.* Fromm International Publishing, 1999.

Johns, Alger F. *A Short Grammar of Biblical Aramaic.* Berrien Springs, MI: Andrews University Press, 1972. Pages 5-7.

Stephen King interview with Stan Nicholls, *SFX Magazine.* No. 45: December 1998.

Gaudiose, Dorothy M. *Prophet of the People: A Biography of Padre Pio.* New York: Alba House, 1977. Page 207.

Harris, William Vernon. *Dreams and Experience in Classical Antiquity.* Harvard University Press, 2009.

Goll, James and Michal Ann. *Dream Language: The Prophetic Power of Dreams, Revelations, and the Spirit of Wisdom.* Shippensburg, PA: Destiny Image Publishers, 2006.

Bloom, Harold. *Mary Wollstonecraft Shelley.* Info Base Publishing, 2008. Page 69.

Jack Nicklaus, as told to a *San Francisco Chronicle* reporter; June 27, 1964.

Kaempffert, Waldemar, ed. The Elias Howe dream story is told in *A Popular History of American Invention* (Volume II). New York: C. Scribner's Sons, 1924. Page 385.

Oldis, Daniel. *The Lucid Dream Manifesto* (Reprint of *Lucid Dreams, Dreams and Sleep: Theoretical Constructions*). Bloomington, IN: iUniverse, Inc., 2006. Page 17.

The
DREAMS
Course & Lab*™

Jim
Driscoll

Zach
Mapes

The Dreams Course is a two day course dedicated to teaching the process, theory, and framework of dream interpretation.

*The Dreams Lab is 2 days of actively working through dreams from the class and selected examples. Recommended prerequisite is the Dreams Course or completion of *"DREAMS: a biblical model of interpretation"* .

For more information go to : www.thedreamscourse.com